M000105657

THE GOOD DOCTOR

BREAKING THE RULES, MAKING A DIFFERENCE

LANCE O'SULLIVAN

WITH MARGIE THOMSON

PENGUIN BOOKS

PENGUIN

UK | USA | Canada | Ireland | Australia
India | New Zealand | South Africa | China

Penguin is an imprint of the Penguin Random House group of companies,
whose addresses can be found at global.penguinrandomhouse.com.

Penguin
Random House
New Zealand

First published by Penguin Random House New Zealand, 2015

10 9 8 7 6 5 4 3 2 1

Cover and text design by Megan van Staden © Penguin Random House New Zealand
Cover photograph by Jane Ussher
Printed and bound in Australia by Griffin Press, an Accredited ISO AS/NZS 14001
Environmental Management Systems Printer
A catalogue record for this book is available from the National Library of New Zealand.

ISBN 978 0 14 357251 0

penguinrandomhouse.co.nz

CONTENTS

—

INĀ KEI TE MŌHIO KOE KO WAI KOE, I ANGA MAI KOE I HEA, KEI TE MŌHIO KOE. KEI TE ANGA ATU KI HEA

//

IF YOU KNOW WHO YOU ARE AND WHERE YOU ARE FROM, THEN YOU WILL KNOW WHERE YOU ARE GOING

—

PROLOGUE //

—

MAKING A
DIFFERENCE

// TWO PATHWAYS DIVERGE

A couple of teaching staff were chatting in the secondary school staffroom as they got things ready for the lunchtime rush. As one of them poured cups of tea, a thought struck her.

'Whatever happened to that boy, Lance O'Sullivan? I suppose he's in jail by now?'

A third person, who had been my mum's next-door neighbour, overheard the conversation and couldn't resist. 'Oh,' she interrupted. 'Lance is at medical school.'

You could have heard a pin drop.

Everyone thought we O'Sullivan boys were going to jail. That's what a friend of my brother's told us, and I guess it looked that way for a while, more for me than my younger brother, Matt. We were easy marks — the half-caste kids of a solo mother. Matt was high-spirited and mischievous, but by the time he got to college he was a good student. There were probably times he was tarred with the same brush as me, though, because for a few years there my future didn't look bright. I was in serious danger of becoming a statistic:

a Māori boy who was failing at school and, at the age of 12 or so, had already had a brush or two with the law. By 15 I'd been expelled from two schools and I had an attitude problem that was getting me into some pretty vicious fist fights.

No one's going to tell me what to do.

I was called a nigger by my Pākehā neighbours, and a honky by my Māori cousins. I was a pretty confused kid. Was I black or was I white? I was looking for my identity in all the wrong places — among the troublemakers at school, my alcoholic father. Which way was my life going to go? The path I was on was leading me straight to failure.

The one thing that got me off that path and onto the right track was being able to make a different choice about my identity. I found myself, at the age of 15, in a Māori environment for the first time, surrounded by strong, positive Māori role models, with te reo flying all around me. I discovered there is a lot to be proud of in being a Māori man — and then I found this huge thirst to know more.

That's why I think my story is worth telling. I hope it'll inspire other young people with the idea that you don't have to follow pathways that seem set in stone. You can dream and achieve. My story is one of making a go of things — and also a story about the value of knowing who you are, and of contributing to the community and the country. It's about help coming along at just the right time.

As I learned more about my own identity and began to find out about the history of my people, and the realities of life for many Māori today — Māori men, for instance, have a life expectancy that's 14 years less than non-Māori men; rheumatic fever, a lethal but preventable disease, has almost disappeared in Pākehā children but our rates for Māori and Pasifika children are among the highest in the developed world — I was filled with a passion to help improve the situation for my people.

When I found my identity, I also found my self-belief and my purpose. But I still had no idea how I was going to make my contribution.

//

I could be a doctor, they said. But I knew no doctors. No one in my family — not one of hundreds of cousins on my dad's side — had ever been to university, let alone medical school. But against all the odds, I'd gone from being a drop-out to runner-up dux of Hato Petera College, and my future was now looking bright. My schoolteachers were encouraging me to think big: doctor, lawyer.

But medical school's really hard! Smart people go there — people who aren't like me.

Then one day my Auntie Nellie, my father's sister, called me.

'Nephew,' she said — that was how she talked to me — 'Nephew, I'd like you to come with me to a hui.'

I was 17, and the hui was on a Friday night.

'What is it, Auntie?' I asked cautiously.

'It's a hui on rongoā Māori, traditional Māori healing.'

'OK,' I said reluctantly.

I could see that I might find it useful, since people were saying I could be a doctor. So I went along to a marae in Māngere called Mataatua and it's lucky I did, because something really important happened. A young Māori man stood up to address the hui and it turned out he was a doctor. He was in his mid-twenties, he spoke fluent Māori, elegant English. He was smart, he was charismatic, and he captured my heart. I couldn't stop staring.

W*ow*, I thought. *I'm going to be like you. I'm going to be a Māori doctor who can stand and speak with a lot of confidence and snare people's attention.*

I was inspired, and I was aware of a thought leaping into life inside me:

I want to inspire others just like you've inspired me.

That man was in my life for 45 minutes — when I talk about him in presentations I call him the '45-minute Man' — but he changed my life. *To be like him,* that goal was sitting at the peak of the maunga I was going to climb.

The time I spent listening to him had a huge impact on me, and it taught me that if I could give an hour to others, as he did, who knows what amazing things could follow. When we lead by example, we can have a big effect on the world.

So it was settled: that's what I was going to do. I was going to show leadership like him. I was going to go to medical school and — somehow — make a contribution to my people.

He was the first Māori doctor that I'd ever seen. I didn't know they existed. I didn't know it was possible. And I get told that now, too, even 25 years later.

We didn't know there were any like you.

//

Fast forward about 15 years and I'm in Kaitāia running echocardiograms on schoolchildren as part of a Heart Foundation screening programme to detect heart disease caused by undiagnosed rheumatic fever. Of 870 kids, we found eight whose heart valves were diseased. Seven of them will have to have painful monthly penicillin injections until they're 21 (and at least one of those, a young boy who has quite bad heart damage, is so afraid of the nurse with that needle that he now refuses the treatment, meaning he will almost certainly experience cardiac problems in his twenties and thirties).

The only option for one boy, Michael Paraha, was open-heart surgery. No one knew he'd been sick. Finding Michael was fantastic on the one hand because if his condition hadn't been picked up, he would have turned up at a hospital emergency department in his twenties, struggling to breathe because of gross and significant heart failure. But in every other sense it was sad and an indictment on our health system that our young children suffer such preventable health complications.

IF OUR YOUNG PEOPLE AREN'T HEALTHY, OUR FUTURE ISN'T EITHER.

The surgery took place two years later when Michael was 13, and I went down to Auckland's Starship Hospital to observe, so that I could burn into my heart and memory the nature of this illness. To see one of our kids get his chest opened up, seeing his heart laid out, ravaged by disease . . . it was terrible. And for Michael, it's a legacy for life. He came through the physical aspects of the surgery quite well. But there are ongoing concerns for someone of that age going through such major surgery — there is an open question about the impact of it on his life. It's likely he will need further operations in the future.

This is what drives me. If our young people aren't healthy, our future isn't either.

My wife Tracy and I have seven children — wonderful, beautiful Māori kids who will be an asset to our community and our world. But when we moved to the Far North eight years ago, we found that too many families and too many children couldn't get to the doctor and couldn't get their medicine because it was all too expensive. Too many kids, like Michael, were being damaged by illnesses that are easily preventable, leaving them unable to reach their potential in life. What a loss to them as individuals, and to New Zealand as a country.

Now my job here is in the trenches, in the mud, doing the grind, day in, day out, and I love it because I know I am making a difference. I am finding ways to improve the health of my people by understanding and respecting the community that exists up here in Kaitāia and the Far North. We are doing this through the health clinic that Tracy and I set up just two years ago, and through the health measures and education scholarships we have set up through our MOKO Foundation.

It's all about taking a health leadership role in our community.

//

I've been involved in a couple of issues that have hit the national headlines — rightly so, as they illustrate the reality of child poverty in our country.

I was in the clinic one day when I got a phone call from a mother whose child had overdosed on antibiotics.

'Bring your child in,' I said.

'I can't get to the clinic,' she replied.

So I went to her house and I was able to see exactly what had happened. I opened her fridge and there was absolutely nothing in it except a whole lot of blue medicine bottles: paracetamol, antibiotics, calamine lotion. There was no food. The hungry child had gone to the fridge and drank a whole lot of antibiotics, even though the taste was disgusting. The child was fine, but what was really stark for me was that this was no accident — it was a preventable incident. And the situation just goes to show the value of house calls.

On another occasion I went to pick up my car from the local mechanic. It was around election time, and the mechanic said to me: 'Lance, who is the best one to vote for to deal with child poverty?'

He explained that the previous night he'd seen some people at the back of his car yard. He assumed they were up to no good, and he yelled at them to get the hell out of there. But as he came closer, what he saw shocked him. It was a group of kids, aged maybe eight or nine, and they were foraging through his pig bucket, taking food.

When he asked them why, the kids responded that they were hungry.

We brought this to the attention of the local child services, and then the media got involved. One well-known interviewer said to me: 'Come on, Lance, we're not the worst. There are people in Cambodia who have far worse poverty than we do.'

But the point is, we're not in Cambodia. We're in New Zealand and we are proud to be a country which we think should give everyone an equal start and equal opportunities.

I believe the general public aren't happy to hear there are children living in poverty in New Zealand.

Some people claim this is solely a matter of individual responsibility, and it's true some parents are not good at looking after their kids. But my response is that children don't have an option; they don't have a choice. They can't choose how much beer their parents are going to drink, how many cigarettes their parents are going to smoke. We have to support those in need when no one else will.

I am the son of a solo mother who was the beneficiary of a welfare state that showed care and compassion. The rewards to the country from supporting vulnerable people are great. I'm not talking about a career of support, not a lifetime of support, but in that moment when someone needs our help, we should be a nation of compassionate people who say: *We will help you get through this time of hardship. We believe investing in you will be beneficial for us as a nation.*

//

Leadership is about inspiration. It's about making those around me feel better about themselves and more excited about their potential to contribute. If I talk at a school prize-giving and tell the story of being brought up by a solo mother who was a beneficiary, I know I'm doing my job when a solo mother comes up afterwards and says: 'I'm so inspired because my son just heard you talk and you told him that he also is capable of achieving these things.'

Leadership is about hard work. The leaders I've studied and hold in high regard — Sir Āpirana Ngata, Sir Peter Buck — worked tirelessly for their people, existing on three, four, five hours' sleep a night and sacrificing a lot. I believe that's also a component of leadership. I believe I demonstrate hard work.

Leadership is about challenging those around me. It's easy to challenge those on the other team — the government, the mainstream — but I believe leadership is equally about challenging those close to me, and especially myself.

In fact, the challenge I present to myself, to be a role model to my family and my community, is perhaps the most demanding because there is no let-up. Some would say it's a burden, that you can't pick your nose without someone criticising you, or look at your watch when you're at an event, or ever seem disinterested in what's being said to you. Or swear, or be an idiot. But I revel in that challenge. I've worked very consciously to create the kind of family that I would like to have had as a child, and to be a person my children can be proud of.

I try really hard to demonstrate what I believe in. I try to demonstrate being a good husband, a good father, a good son, a health-conscious Māori doctor.

Here's an example:

I'm at a meeting in Ellerslie, Auckland, dressed in my running shoes and my running gear. Then after the meeting I run to the airport and have a shower at the Koru Lounge. Before I set off after the meeting with my pack on my back, the people I've been talking to, who are all from a mainstream health organisation, are saying, *What are you doing?* The answer is that I'm putting into action what we've just been talking about — a healthy lifestyle. In our health system we have far too many people who will tell you what to do: do as I say, not as I do. I say, 'This is what I'm doing.'

WHEN I TALK TO PĀKEHĀ, OR THOSE WHO LIVE IN DIFFERENT PARTS OF THE COUNTRY, I AM BUILDING A BRIDGE BETWEEN TWO WORLDS.

The Far North is one of the highest needs areas for Māori. Of the 14 schools in the Kaitāia district, none are above decile 3 — in fact, we talk about decile 3 schools as being privileged, the 'haves'. How sad is that? And one of the saddest consequences of our impoverished community is that three out of four Māori children who come to see me in my clinic today will be dead before they are 65.

I'm living in an area that desperately requires leadership, and I try to demonstrate that leadership through the work I do as a doctor, both in my clinic and out and about in our community. This leadership comes from understanding the factors that prevent my people from accessing healthcare and having healthy lifestyles, and doing my best to address not just the symptoms but the causes. There's no point in writing yet another prescription for asthma medication for a child who lives in a home that's leaking, cold and damp, and whose family can't afford proper heating.

I'm by no means the only one. There are many amazing people in the Far North and in other poor communities working hard to give our kids a better start in life, to offset some of the disadvantages dealt to them by history, by poverty and by dysfunctional family environments. I believe that some of the programmes we have implemented here would work in other places around the country.

We need to think differently if we want to change the outcomes.

The awards I have won in the last couple of years have given me a lot to think about. I realise I can influence opinion; I can use my position of being well known to make a difference. I can be a leader.

Yet my pathway to leadership happened by accident rather than by design. What might I have been able to do if I'd had a mentor when I was just starting out, someone to sit with me and advise me? I am passionate about 'designing' our future leaders. That's one of my reasons for writing this book — to inspire young people with the idea that they, too, can make a difference. This is also an important part of the work we do with our MOKO Foundation: giving active support to the leaders of tomorrow.

//

Some people have expressed surprise that I was the recipient of the New Zealander of the Year award when my work, in essence, is quite challenging to the status quo.

The dominant political ideology is every man for themselves, and yet, in my experience, that's not how most people think. I visit a lot of places around this country and talk to those from across the spectrum, and people tell me all the time they are very proud of the work I'm doing. When I talk to Pākehā, or those who live in different parts of the country — in Otago or Tīmaru or Wellington — I am building a bridge between two worlds, the very distinct worlds of Māori and Pākehā. I can speak across the divide, and that is the talent I want to use. It's the legacy I would like to leave. I'm not being confrontational, though I think there are challenging aspects to what I say. But nevertheless my kōrero reaches the hearts and minds of people.

In fact, the work I do means I have to challenge myself as well. I talk about child poverty and I work among very vulnerable people full of unmet needs — and I sometimes have to remind myself that I am now different from them. I am now part of a privileged group: I'm educated. I am a doctor. I have a very good income. But what I find very reassuring is that a lot of New Zealanders, who are also different from the people I serve, support me and are very comfortable with the work I do, because they want a caring society and a fairer society.

//

Most days, I bike home from work. Some days I'm so exhausted I think about taking the car instead, but usually I talk myself out of it.

'IT IS EASIER TO BUILD STRONG CHILDREN THAN IT IS TO REPAIR BROKEN MEN' — FREDERICK DOUGLASS.

You know you'll feel better once you're on your bike.

It's always the right decision. My head clears, my body feels energised and I'm reminded how blessed I am. I ride past the children of Kaitāia and know we're making a difference to their health outcomes and therefore what their potential could be. It's what I went to medical school for.

'It is easier to build strong children than it is to repair broken men' — these are the words of the African-American anti-slavery campaigner Frederick Douglass. He wrote them more than 150 years ago, but it is a truth that guides my work today. Each child is a new opportunity.

HE KĀKANO AHAU I RUIA MAI I RANGIĀTEA

//

I AM A SEED WHICH WAS SOWN IN THE HEAVENS OF RANGIĀTEA

A FAMOUS PROVERB FROM THE AOTEA WAKA, WHICH SHOWS THE IMPORTANCE OF YOUR GENEALOGY AND YOUR CULTURE

PART 1 //

—

WHO I WAS BEFORE I WAS BORN

1 // FATHERHOOD

I have a photo that is one of my most treasured possessions. It's of me and my youngest son, Lance junior, at this time still just a little boy. I am holding him in my arms and we are embracing, and when I look at this photo I see so much more than just me and Lance. We are a father and a son. I am looking into my son's eyes and holding him up high, knowing that he is going to have every opportunity to achieve greatness, to contribute to our people, our society, our country. He's going to be dynamic and energetic, and all those things are so exciting for a father to see.

In return, my son looks into my eyes and knows that he has a father who will provide protection, who will keep him safe and give him advice and direction when it's required. He looks to his father as a role model for how to be a man, a husband, a father. He knows that his father will show him these things.

When it comes to sons and fathers, a son will always look to his dad to find out who he is himself, to find out how to act in the world, what sort of man to be.

This photo is a Kodak moment and it would be fair to

say that not everyone in this country has the opportunity to have such a moment. It certainly wasn't one that I was lucky enough to have with my own father.

//

My father was an alcoholic. Alcohol shaped his life, made him violent and incapable of being a good husband and father. In turn, his life shaped my own.

SOME MEN LOOK TO THEIR FATHERS AND ALL THEY FIND IS ABSENCE.

I've talked to a lot of other guys who were brought up by their mothers, and we're so desperate to be good fathers. Yet we're afraid that we don't know how. We weren't able to look up to our own fathers; we weren't shown how to be men in all the positive meanings of that word. We looked at our fathers and we saw behaviour that hurt. We saw behaviour that damaged ourselves, our siblings and our mothers.

Some men look to their fathers and all they find is absence.

I had quite a lot of contact with my dad compared to others. I would have seen him maybe once a month throughout my childhood, and I know that's a lot more often than some kids see their fathers. My father never denied my existence, and he didn't vanish off the scene for years at a time. Yet I smile as I write that, because the contact I had with him was often poor. I know the pain of not having a father who offers safety, protection, advice.

One of the scariest moments of my life was when I was about

nine. I was in Dad's car — he drove a tiny Morris Minor van, its lights held on with insulation tape — and he was very, very drunk. We were on the Newmarket overpass and he was veering off to the side, zigzagging, almost hitting the barrier, pulling away just in time, veering towards it again. It was terrifying, and again and again I thought, *We're going over the edge.*

I'd wanted so much to see him. I'd rung him up and cried over the phone for him to come and get me, and for once he did. Most often he wouldn't turn up. He took me to watch a game of rugby league at Carlaw Park. It was a cold afternoon and the rain was driving in under the stands, but I was there with my father and I was determined to enjoy myself. He was knocking back Black Heart rum out of a hip flask, and getting really drunk. He wasn't being rough with me, but he was loud and obnoxious and it was very embarrassing.

And then it was into the car for that terrifying ride through Auckland traffic. I was crying. *I want to go home. I'm scared.* Somehow, we didn't die, nobody stopped us, and we finally made it back to his house.

Throughout my life I've been embarrassed by his behaviour, but as a young boy I was also really anxious. Maybe this was the first time I'd been on my own with him when he was like that — mostly there would be other people around, maybe his brothers, who'd all be drinking, and I'd be playing with my cousins and not noticing the men getting drunk.

The next day when I got home to Mum's I didn't say a word about it.

'How was it?'

'Good.'

Even though I'd been so scared, there was no way I would ever tell Mum, because I didn't want her to stop me going back again. I loved my dad.

I couldn't understand why my mother left my father. It was really hard for me to understand when I was four, when I was

10, when I was 12, and then 15, having problems with my life.

Why did you take me away from my father?

And this is what I see all the time in my work. We'll be caring for a little kid who's been hurt or neglected by a parent, and someone will always ask, *How can they love that parent?* But children have this sincere, authentic love for their parents. Sure, it's often misplaced, but they are immature little things who haven't developed a critical way of thinking.

Dad would often let me down.

'Hey, Lance, I'm coming to pick you up and we're going away to your grandmother's for the weekend.'

He wouldn't turn up.

'Hey, Lance, I'm going to come and watch your league game. Where is it?'

The whole time I was warming up, and then when the game had started and I was on the field, my thoughts were more focused on the sideline to see if he had turned up.

He rarely turned up.

'Hey, Lance, I'll come and get you and we'll do this and this and this.'

And perhaps he would actually turn up and I'd get in the car all excited, but on the way to wherever we were supposed to be going we'd stop at one of his favourite pubs, say the Manukau Arms near Māngere Bridge, and out he'd get. I'd stay in the car until it got dark and scary. Sometimes I got so bored I'd take the car for a spin around the block — I was about 12 when I started doing that. Finally I would have to go into the pub to try to drag him out.

It was equally dark and scary inside those bars. I walked past all these pissed people, sitting there with their jugs, until I found Dad and he introduced me to a whole lot of 'aunties'.

'Hey son, this is your auntie.'

I was like, 'I've never seen her before. How can she be my auntie?'

But I had to put up with smoochy kisses from these giggling, drunk-as people going, 'Cor, you're such a handsome fulla. You sure he's your father?'

Dad'd be like, 'Here's some money, go and buy some chips and wait in the car.'

I was in and out of the pub until he was ready to go. Finally he'd come out, really drunk and obnoxious, and I'd drive him home through the Auckland traffic. Or, worse, he drove.

It wasn't that he was treating me like a mate rather than the small boy I was. I actually don't think I was high on his priorities; I didn't register.

Sometimes he turned up out of the blue, wanting to take me somewhere. But if it was unplanned, Mum wouldn't let me go. She protected me heaps. I didn't see it as protection then, but she was the gate-keeper quite a lot. For good reason.

Certainly, my habits when I first started drinking reflected what I'd learned from Dad. Sometimes he took me away for the weekend to his little house in Glen Innes, and I sat at home with some videos and some Peanut Slabs while he went out and got drunk. When he came home I'd be asleep in his room, or trying to sleep, while him and his mates would fight and muck around and swear. It was horrible. But when I began drinking I was exactly like that myself. I was a 13-year-old kid drinking out of a plastic cask of wine — it tasted revolting, but I was with a bunch of other kids and it was supposed to be fun. I started getting drunk and I started behaving like my father. I even spoke like him too.

This is what my mum was protecting me from. I saw my dad behave like that 20, 30, 50 times in my life — imagine if I'd seen it 500 times. Imagine if I'd seen my mother getting beaten up every other week, like some of the women I see in my clinic. Sometimes the only thing that separates good people from bad people is how much they've been exposed to badness. And, of course, how much of the other stuff you've seen: stability, routine, respect, cooperation. I'd see my father maybe once a month, maybe less — I felt it depended on a few things like how much his partner liked me that month. The rest of the time I was with Mum, and that saved me.

2 // THE JOINING OF TWO RIVERS

My personal story began the night my mother Marlene — just 18, not long out of her private Catholic boarding school and feeling rebellious — went to a party and became smitten with a charming, handsome Māori freezing worker who was drinking there with his mates.

The party was in Tīmaru, which was where Marlene had grown up on her parents' sheep farm. My grandfather, Brendan O'Sullivan, qualified for a rehabilitation loan from the government when he returned from World War Two after fighting in Guadalcanal. It was a chance to buy land. The soldiers from Guadalcanal were some of the last back to the country once peace was declared, and most of the best land had already been taken. But Grandad looked hard and finally settled on a 484 acre plot of gorse-covered land, partly rolling hills, partly flat, in South Canterbury. He married Margaret, and together they worked extraordinarily hard to clear the land and to establish a living on it, at which they were very successful. Brendan and Margaret were talented farmers, highly esteemed by the local community, and people from Lincoln College used to come to them to discuss farming issues. My mother's family was middle class, stable, conservative in that South Canterbury way. They had a very safe and comfortable life, and Mum and her sister and brothers were on a pathway of education and opportunity. Mum, though, was unsettled and a rebel in her teens, and had already dropped out of nursing training.

Dad — Eddy — was just passing through on his motorbike with three mates, working his way around the country, freezing works by freezing works.

He had grown up near Thames in the North Island — one of 18 children living on a small rural property. His grandfather had returned from World War One and, rather than being welcomed back with the chance to purchase cheap land, found his ancestral land had shrunk due to legislative change, heavy rates and suchlike. By the time Eddy's parents, Mita and Maggie Watene, were bringing up their 18 children, 15 of whom survived into adulthood, on the remaining land at Kōpū, they were living in poverty, struggling to eke a living out of their garden. They ate dog bones because it was all they could afford, and for years my dad's sisters thought Champion was a clothing brand, because that was printed on the flour sacks from which Maggie made their clothes. They had a saying — first home on a Friday afternoon was best dressed for Friday night.

After Mita died in his early fifties of a heart attack the family fell apart. He had been a heavy drinker and there are varied accounts of him; some people say he was a gambler, a womanising wife-basher, and others that he was a staunch and devout Mormon who loved his family, worked hard and treated them all with respect. Perhaps he was a bit of both, at different stages of his life. At any rate, Eddy had grown up with what we would now term social and probably cultural dysfunction.

So when my mother met my father, it was very much the joining of two rivers.

Lots of the Tīmaru girls liked the Māori boys, with their open manner, their humour and their music. Mum remembers that when she was just a girl a Māori man came to work on their farm as a fencer. She was fascinated — he was colourful, played the guitar, sang, painted. So when she met Eddy he reminded her of the man she'd known years before, only Eddy had the added bonus of being handsome and young. He would have been all Brylcreemed up, very much the life and soul of the party.

She took him home to meet her parents. They liked Eddy. It was hard not to — he was engaging and well mannered. Marlene was quickly struck by Eddy's respect for his own mother, illustrated by the amount of money he sent her every week. Because he worked out of town at the freezing works he was unable to get to the post office, so he asked Marlene to send the money order through each time. It was half his pay packet. He knew his mother's widow's pension wasn't enough to bring up the little ones still at home. Eddy was generous and thoughtful.

Yet at a deeper level Marlene's parents were horrified, and that was more about social discrimination than racism. The divide was too much. They were middle class, Catholic, rural, and he was lower class, poor, Māori. Different social class. Different values.

But Marlene and Eddy began going out together, and when the Tīmaru works closed for the season and Eddy headed back up north, Marlene went with him.

While he got other freezing-works jobs, she did a variety of casual work — in hotels as housemaid or cook, or for a dentist. Much to the horror of Mum's extended whānau, they didn't marry. In her family, you didn't do things like live with someone without getting married. But for Marlene and Eddy, the subject just didn't come up and they remained de facto. Mum was 21 when they had their first child, my sister Nikki. Two years and 10 months later, I arrived, born at National Women's Hospital in Auckland. Our brother Matt came four years later, but by the time he was born Mum had left Dad, briefly partnering with Matt's dad, and then striking out on her own.

From early on, the signs were there that Eddy had a drinking problem. Mum's brother would say to her, 'Surely you can see this side of him? Can't you see it?' But she was in love, didn't see the signs, and so the problem progressed. Eddy, of course, had been shaped by his own background, and Marlene never felt judgemental towards him. *How would I have turned out if I'd had to walk in his shoes?* she asked herself.

Then the question arises: in this meeting between the middle-class, educated girl and the young Māori man, who was already on the pathway to a drinking problem and who came from a dysfunctional background, who was going to have the greatest impact on the relationship?

It was obvious quite soon that Eddy's influence would win out. Over time their relationship became defined by his violence towards Mum, his heavy drinking and his gambling. This resulted in Mum not having enough money to feed us, despite working part-time. And for Marlene it was made harder because she was now detached from her family base, living in Auckland among Eddy's family.

My dad's family were quite well known in the criminal world. Most of my uncles — and there were five or six of them — and Dad had been in jail. They weren't in a formal gang but they were very feared in Auckland. They ran bookmaking and standover and confidence stuff. One of my uncles in particular was a very prominent figure in the criminal world there. Recently I attended a prison where I gave a motivational talk to young Māori inmates. It was not my first time in prison. My mother told me that my sister and I would go with her to visit my dad in Mount Eden prison when I was a preschooler. As children, we were often exposed to acts of violence against my mother. There was no security and a lot of instability.

So that was the life.

//

Finally, a friend of Mum's walked into our house late one night. It was after 11 p.m. and there were a lot of people in the lounge, mostly quite intoxicated — they'd probably come back after the pub closed — and little Nikki, who must have been about five or six, was still up and serving beer to the grown-ups. Mum's friend said to her the next day, 'Hey, this is not a good situation. You need to be thinking about what effect this is going to have on your kids in the long term.'

Mum always had a strong idea that she wanted to raise her children to be, in her words, 'well-adjusted young citizens who had a contribution to make in society'. It was her mantra, but for a while, when she was struggling in her relationship with Eddy, she lost sight of that. Her friend reminded her, challenged her to remember, and Mum knew she had to leave Eddy for our sake.

As Mum says, she could have chosen to stay with Eddy and tried to help him through his drinking problem, but she chose instead to take Nikki and me and go. She knew that the risk to us of being in that environment was just too great. It's not a risk you can take for your kids. She knew she had to get out of there.

Mum never had any regrets. It must have been hard at times, especially as her next relationship with Matt's dad didn't last. I went through a stage of being angry with her for taking me away from my dad. I was only about four at the time we left and I don't remember much about the bad things that happened. So I'd say to her, *Why did you do this to me? Why did you take me away from my father?* It was really difficult for me to understand.

———

THE DOMESTIC PURPOSES BENEFIT HAD ONLY EXISTED SINCE 1972. WITHOUT IT, MY MOTHER WOULD NOT HAVE BEEN ABLE TO LEAVE THE SITUATION SHE WAS IN.

Mum's greatest fear for me was that I would go back to Dad's family. She dreaded the possibility that I would end up like him, be drawn to him, his family and the way they lived. And, in fact, that was a very strong pull. But she gave me my best chance at a different life when she left him.

Kids often wish their parents would get back together again, and sometimes that does work, but it's only really possible if there have been some necessary changes, and I'm afraid that with Dad it never happened.

//

After Mum left our father, it wasn't long before she bought a house in the eastern suburbs of Auckland where, at that time, you could count on one hand how many Māori or dark-skinned people lived in the community. We were very lucky — Mum's parents gave her some money to help with a deposit on a house so that we could have the stability and safety of our own home, and we moved into a new subdivision in a cul-de-sac in Highland Park, between Pakūranga and Howick. As long as Mum could pay the mortgage and the rates, it was ours. And that's where we lived for my entire childhood.

This was the 1970s, and Mum was a Pākehā mother raising three half-caste children alone (Matt's dad was also Māori), in a time and place that didn't much like solo parents, or Māori. The Domestic Purposes Benefit (DPB) had only existed since 1972. Without it, my mother would not have been able to leave the situation she was in. However, it was still a contentious issue and solo mothers were frowned upon by many people.

Then, as now, beneficiaries were the sub-class — unable to partake in many of the activities that are a normal part of life for other people. Unless you've got other support, or other sources of income, those relying on a benefit are unable to give their kids what they actually need. So, to supplement her DPB, Mum earned extra money cleaning houses. It was illegal, but it was the difference, she'd say, between living or just existing. It meant we could take part in sports and that she could take us to rare cultural events, to expand our horizons.

Mum knew the importance of education, and she differentiated between education and schooling. She used to say to us: 'School is part of your education. I'm responsible for the rest, and if I can't answer your questions then I need to find somebody who can.' So as much as she could she introduced us to sport and music and the arts, albeit on a limited basis. She dragged us to an art exhibition and when we were bored stupid she said, 'Find one painting you like and stand in front of it.' She dragged us to a musical and when we said we hated it she said, 'Find one song you like and think about that.'

This is what I'm really proud of about my mother: she put us first.

She didn't have men coming into our lives who we had to call uncle. Calling one guy 'uncle' one month, and another guy 'uncle' the next month is something I see every day in some of the families I work with. With Mum, I see a woman who sacrificed companionship, comfort, even the material benefits of being with another man, for her children.

Mum gave us the best life she could. She always considered us first. She didn't drink, didn't smoke. I came home from school and she was there. She lost her rag at times, she smacked us often, but when I think about trying to raise kids like me and my brother and sister — though I was definitely the hardest — I think she did a great job.

If I was grumpy in the morning she'd say, 'Give it away, please. I don't want my day dampened by someone not being happy in the morning.'

Mum was a greenie way before everyone else — not that she would have called herself that. She would have just said she was frugal. Her priority was always to pay the mortgage and rates, and everything else came second to that. She baked her own bread, and made our lunches with it. When it was lunchtime at school I'd be all shy because everyone else had their Tip Top sliced. I'd go round the corner and eat it because I was embarrassed. The other kids would tease me: 'You guys can't afford proper bread!' But that bread — I can taste it today. It was awesome. Fresh, home-baked brown bread.

We didn't have a car when I was young. Cars are expensive to buy and run, and we didn't have that kind of disposable income. Instead, we biked everywhere. Sometimes for a treat we went to the movies, all riding there on our bikes, wearing our safety jackets, carrying a packed lunch to eat inside the cinema. We rarely saw fizzy drink and junk food. We caught the bus into town so we could march down Queen Street against nukes, and Mum would go out on the boats protesting against the US frigates.

We didn't have a TV for ages, so we read heaps. When we did get a TV it was a crappy old black and white one that we had right into my teens.

It was all real good stuff. I look back on it and think: *amazing*. Mum worked so hard to make a good life for us.

She hadn't been to university and, being a rebel, had dropped out of nursing training, but she always believed that knowledge is power. She told us, 'There are two things that create power: one is money; the other is knowledge.' She used to say, 'I'm not likely to have money but there's one thing I can acquire.' And she went out and learned as much as she could. We used to laugh at her and call her a course junkie. She did a community work certificate at Manukau Institute of Technology (MIT), riding to Ōtara with my little brother on the back of her bike, about 15 kilometres each way, through the Auckland traffic. She did a certificate in community studies at the Continuing Education Department at Auckland University. She did a course in psycho-cybernetics, which is about training the mind, based on the book by self-help author Maxwell Maltz. In later years she did Landmark Forum courses and neurolinguistic programming — always hungry to learn more about the human mind.

Mum also did lots of voluntary work in the local community, working with the city council, MIT and local people to improve the resources in our area. By the time we were all at high school she was off the DPB and working full-time as a cleaner. Mum had work coming out her ears. She was such a good cleaner she even had a waiting list of people wanting her services, but she knew she couldn't keep cleaning for ever — it's really tough on the body. Sometimes if her back was bad I'd help her by doing the hard stuff, like the vacuuming and mopping the floors.

Once we'd all left home, she did a foundation course at Auckland University, as well as a writing course, and then, at the age of 55, she became a full-time student, enrolling to do a Bachelor of Health Science. By that stage all of us kids had qualifications, and she wanted one, too. Even though she was a full-time student she was still cleaning full-time. It was hard yakka but she had a mission: to get a degree in three years. She did it, and got her first 'real' job at 60, working in community public health in Tīmaru, then health promotion in Counties Manukau, and that's where she worked for the next five years, right up until the time she came to Kaitāia to support me and Tracy in our work.

It was never her intention to retire early, but she did it for us. She's still got heaps of energy to give.

From Mum and her family I learned so much about the importance of hard work and sacrifice. She raised us under tough circumstances and she taught us about community; that we have an obligation to think of others above ourselves. Right from childhood, we were engaged in robust discussions and debates about stuff like that.

There were times, when I was in my angry stage, that I would challenge her as a Pākehā, blame her, and we might go to bed feeling a bit frosty. But actually, because of her background she has lots of insight to offer that's relevant to the work we do now; she brings a Pākehā view to the things we discuss, and all her depth of understanding of health promotion, and that's really good. My mum is a bit like Tracy — very grounded. I accuse them of being brutal realists and stifling me, whereas I want to be fancy-free and have big ideas. But it's a good balance.

//

If I wasn't a doctor I'd like to be a farmer, maybe in the South Island. I'd be happy being a sheep farmer way down there, although I think I'd be content anywhere rural. I had this dream that by age 50 I'd be 50 per cent medicine and 50 per cent farming. If a farmer heard me saying that they'd probably scoff. *He thinks it's like that, does he? That anyone can just walk off the street and be a farmer?* I do realise farming is complex, but if I had enough land it would be fantastic. I'd put my Red Bands on one day and my stethoscope the next. Spiritually it would complete me.

Even though I was a city boy, I got my affinity for the rural life as a young kid when, every year until I was 15, Mum took us down to her parents' sheep farm in Tīmaru. We were there for at least a month, sometimes two, over the Christmas holidays, and occasionally we'd go down at other times of the year as well. That's where Mum's heart was, and ours too, then. It wasn't just her parents; her sister and brothers all lived there with their kids, so for us it was a huge extended-family experience.

This was the other reason we lived so thriftily, because Mum was saving to get us down south. Our grandmother, whom we called Nana, would say to Mum: 'Come to stay for a month to offset your costs, and you're not allowed to pay for anything while you're here.' So as soon as school broke up for the Christmas holidays, we were on our way.

Initially we flew from Auckland to Wellington or Christchurch, then got a little fixed-wing propeller aircraft to Tīmaru. When that became too expensive we switched to the train. We caught the Northerner to Wellington, then hopped on the interisland ferry, then the rail car from Picton to Christchurch, which was really uncomfortable but there was amazing scenery, then finally a bus to Tīmaru. Mum packed food for us to eat, but when we got to the central railway station at Wellington we were allowed to buy something to eat, which was a real novelty, and then again on the ferry when we got a pie.

I loved our grandparents. Though they were conservative South Canterbury farmers, I never felt judged by them. They were good, decent people. My grandmother was kind; my grandfather (known to us all as 'Brenny') was quiet but strong. He would be out working hard while Nana stayed at home getting the dinner ready and looking after the cows and the kids. You rarely heard my grandfather swear. He and Mum's brothers might have a few beers or some whisky — but it was very controlled drinking. They were dedicated to their church, and going to Mass on Sunday was an expectation for all of us, although back in Auckland we didn't usually go. There was an ice cream after if we were good.

I guess you'd say they were old school, significantly shaped by their war service, and I was lucky to have that bedrock in my life. Also, they were generous and, really, they gave us a life. It was because of them that Mum had a house and didn't have a landlord to worry about. They always treated Mum with a lot of respect.

The life I experienced on the farm, and my grandparents' strong values and ethics, gave me a solid platform in my life, and when I later built my Māori identity I had a foundation that had been laid for me by my mother and her family.

I never ever felt any judgement for being Māori. Sometimes my uncles might say 'horis' or use the 'n' word — not about us, just in conversation — and that was uncomfortable. Those terms create a sense of difference, of antipathy, just as if I was to call Pākehā kids 'little white pricks', but it was unthinking rather than intentionally abusive.

I remember one of my uncles calling us little black bastards. But that was unusual, and on that occasion he was angry because we'd done something wrong with the animals — let the sheep out, probably. I wouldn't want to exaggerate those things, though. We loved it down there on the farm, and we felt loved. We had an amazing life with our grandparents and for me, as a boy, it was so good to see the way my uncles worked hard and then could sometimes be playful, silly and fun.

The house itself was a simple homestead but it had everything it needed to make it warm and welcoming. It was up a long farm drive, with a corrugated-iron fence. The garage smelt of birds' nests, and sacking hung under the roof to catch the bird poop so it wouldn't fall on the car. In the implements shed the smell was of diesel and oil that had spilled in patches on the floor.

In the mornings I woke up to magpies calling outside my window, and I hopped out of bed, always keen for the busyness of a farming day, or the sheer fun of life in the country where there's a river to swim and fish in. When you're farming, everybody has a job to do. At home in Auckland it was my job to mow our lawn with the push mower — I had to oil it and service it. I had the same job on the farm, but there we had an old motor mower, a self-drive, and it took ages. I collected eggs every day, and then did the rounds with Brenny checking the sheep.

I loved being out with my grandfather, either walking, him with his shepherd's crook, or on the four-wheel-drive, checking on the stock — are there any lame animals, are any sheep lambing, are any in trouble? I saw life and death. If a lamb was breech, Grandad and my uncles would save its life.

I was intrigued and curious about death. I'd say to my grandfather, 'Let's go and find some dead sheep.' We'd go out and find some, and throw the smelly sheep in the truck then down the offal pit. Even today I've got what Tracy calls a morbid curiosity. We often take our ute up north towards Cape Rēinga or down to Ahipara on Ninety Mile Beach, and as we drive along we see heaps of dead things — whales, sharks, seals, dolphins. I'll always stop and show the kids. It's the only time you get to see these creatures in such detail.

It's the story that gets me. What happened to the sheep, shark, seal? On the farm I was fascinated by the story of the sheep that went wool-blind — when wool got into its eyes it couldn't see, so it stumbled around and got caught up in some bracken where it died. Or the sheep that went lame and fell over and couldn't get up and the magpies got into it, or the hawks. Or the ewe that died trying to give birth to its lamb. Or sometimes I went to the farm in the winter holidays, and we would help the animals which got caught in bad weather. Behind every tragedy there was a story.

One of the highlights of my time on the farm was going with Grandad to butcher the sheep. If we had shearers coming in we needed a lot of meat. If we were doing hay baling we might have quite a few people around and they needed a hot lunch. Or even just feeding the whole family.

We'd go up to the woolshed and he'd tell me not to look while he cut the sheep's throat. 'It's too gory,' he said. But I always sneaked a look. Then he hung the animal up and disembowelled it and gave me the innards to take back to the farmhouse — the lungs, heart, liver, intestines and the bladder — and I sat with Nana as she explained it all to me, how everything worked. Nana had been a nurse on a hospital ship during the war, bringing back wounded soldiers from North Africa, so she knew all about biology. Mum reckons those experiences lay behind my desire to get into medicine, and it probably had an influence, although at the time I just thought I'd like to be a butcher, or a builder. (Nana was really proud when I graduated from medical school, and gave me a picture of Fabiola, the fourth-century patron of nursing.)

We'd have big family picnics at the river with Mum's sister and brothers and all their kids. My grandfather taught us how to skim rocks with the flattest stones, and we made open barbecues, putting river stones in a circle, collecting firewood from the riverbanks and cooking sausages on a hotplate. We camped at the river — real basic camping — or just visited it every day to fish and swim. All those wonderful things.

In the evenings we said our prayers with Nana, kneeling on the carpet by the side of the bed.

I'd roam around the farm collecting interesting things, and by the time I had to go back to Auckland I had filled a little tea box with my treasures, with things like sparrows' and starlings' eggs that we'd blown the yolks out of. If I was lucky I had a hawk's egg. I had wool from the sheep that we'd seen Grandad shearing. Sometimes if I was really lucky I found some merino wool. I had sheep's teeth taken from skulls that I'd found. And ear tags as well. We were there for the cropping too, so I collected plastic bags of barley and wheat kernels. When I got back to Auckland I was so sad, but I took my box of things in to school for show and tell, and I planted the barley and the wheat in our little garden.

Being down there on the farm was special to all us kids. It's funny — I don't remember Nikki so much from my young years. As my older sister she was more like a second mother. I often say that I was raised by two strong women, and one of them was my sister. Even when I'd gone to boarding school in my teens and she was already working, she'd send me parcels of food and goodies. But now we're adults we are close, and we're very aligned in our shared passionate interest in Māori culture and social issues.

Matt and I had a really cool relationship as kids. We were always playing together, war games, that sort of thing. Boy stuff. I think when I was getting into trouble it was hard for him. I wasn't the big brother he could be proud of; but then later, when things were going well for me, our relationship picked up again. Matt's been very successful in his chosen field, advertising and marketing. It's frustrating but he's better than me at a lot of sports — I'm beaten by my little brother at squash and tennis, even though I've been playing them longer. I'm lucky to have Nikki and Matt, and they've been incredibly supportive of me through tough times and through good times.

And then, many years ago, Mum told us about the baby she'd had prior to us. She gave that child up for adoption —

Annita, who lives in Holland with her adoptive parents. We had always wondered about the baby photo that Mum kept in her bedroom, and when Mum told us about Annita we were all so happy to be able to include her in our whānau. We don't see a lot of each other, but she has come out and stayed with us, and it seems very easy that she's now a part of our family, too.

I probably took our farming holiday experiences all for granted until, soon after we'd met, I took Tracy down to meet Nana and Grandad.

Tracy said to me, 'You know you're really lucky, eh?'

I was surprised. 'Why?' I asked. I was thinking, how can she say that, coming as she does from a wealthy background? 'But you guys had cars and video players and all those things.'

'Yeah,' she said, 'but look what you used to *do*.'

And I was like, 'You're right.'

When they sold the family farm we were devastated. It got into financial difficulty a few years before Nana and Brenny died. But we still have all our memories, and for me it was formative. Thanks to my grandparents I grew up in rural New Zealand, and not just in a cul-de-sac in Pakūranga. I was shaped by the open spaces, the beautiful landscapes, the people who lived there.

//

My other rural experiences came on rarer occasions when I visited my father's family at Kōpū, near Thames.

Their land had shrunk to a 2 acre block right next to a creek that was quite a special part of the family history. It's where my dad and my uncles and aunties bathed. It was where they washed their clothes. A couple of their siblings had died there. The creek was a powerful thing, and every five years it flooded over the property and the water came close to the house.

My grandmother had a plain home but it was always very warm and safe. When my uncles were visiting, they wouldn't drink around my grandmother, and the aunties who lived at home were very religious. We'd be doing prayers next to the La-Z-Boy in the lounge, or at the dinner table. Mormon prayers. It was a simple life. They didn't have a farm to run. They didn't have a lot of income. The whole lot of them shared one car.

When we went down to Kōpū, we swam in the creek and went eeling. But at times, playing with my cousins, it was a little bit awkward. They called me 'honky' and I thought that sucked. It was quite a Māori environment and I found it a bit foreign.

I suppose that when we visited it would be because of some special occasion and there would be heaps of people around. When they wanted to feed us they'd roll out the newsprint paper across the big table and put out a whole massive pot of porridge. We'd be sitting outside and it was a real communal meal, all the aunties, all the uncles, all the cousins, the grandmother — so maybe 30 or 40 people. And it would go on for several days.

Thinking about how it was for me as a young boy visiting my dad's family, I reflect that even though there were hard parts to my upbringing there was much about the life my mother created for us that, in comparison to my father's family, was very privileged and generous. Perhaps I was even a bit spoiled, because when I went into that other environment, I really felt the difference. I was there for Christmas one year. There weren't many presents, and I spent most of the day cleaning a drain. *Man, this sucks.* I was used to a feeling of celebration and excitement lasting all day.

It wasn't that they weren't loving to me, or that I didn't feel safe, but the feeling in the house wasn't what I was used to. I believe one of the biggest challenges for my father's family was a poverty of spirit, a feeling that they had been beaten down. That's what I witnessed a lot, and it manifested itself in all sorts of ways, from the sheer simplicity of their life through to the significant social chaos that would go on with the drinking and other problems among my dad's siblings up in Auckland. As a boy I could detect that there was quite a difference between my mother's family and my father's family, and understanding that difference has been one of the main motivations in the life and work that I've chosen for myself.

//

Running along the banks of the creek at Kōpū, between the water and the house, were thick growths of harakeke. Years down the track Tracy and I took some cuttings from that flax and we grow it up here at our home in the Far North, and I like that link back to my grandmother.

So those were the influences on me as I grew up — Pākehā and Māori, middle class and extremely poor. As I grew into teenagerhood it became increasingly difficult for me to bridge these different worlds.

3 // TROUBLEMAKER

Despite Mum's best efforts, by the time I was about eight or nine I was starting to fail. Teachers began to label me as a troublemaker and my reputation was preceding me, from class to class, and then from primary school to intermediate to college.

When a kid is getting into trouble at school and is on a trajectory towards failure, we have to ask the question: What is failing? Is it the student or the system?

When I was in the fourth form, a teacher sat my mother down and said, with absolute sincerity, that I was a slow learner. Other teachers complained to Mum that I was hyperactive, and every now and then someone would suggest to her that I should get put on medication. She would never even consider that. She didn't see me as hyperactive, or even difficult — just very busy. It took a bit to manage me, but she knew I was not a bad kid. 'Harmless strife' is how she described it. Not paying attention, playing where and when I wasn't supposed to. I wasn't intentionally bad, but the upshot was that I was put in a box marked 'trouble'. Have you ever seen a photo of a kid with a dunce's hat on? That was me — made to sit in the corner, always being sent to the principal, getting the strap so many times I lost count.

I was really into war. I used to love war movies and war figurines and war books. Even today I like to learn about World War One and World War Two, the history of the conflicts. But obviously, as a boy, I just liked the conflict.

I made wooden guns and took them to school and organised kids into teams, playing down the back of the fields, all shooting at each other — 'bang, bang!' I got the strap for that in front of the whole school, all the kids looking at me, and the teacher strapped me so hard I cried. I didn't understand what I'd done that was so wrong. I'd got some boys together to play war. I wasn't graffitiing or beating people up or stealing.

___

HAVE YOU EVER SEEN A PHOTO OF A KID WITH A DUNCE'S HAT ON? THAT WAS ME.

Mum did her best to challenge the schools in a constructive way. For instance, one day our class was walking back to school from a short trip and on the way back I went into a playground and fell, banging my head. But because I had done something I wasn't supposed to I had to keep walking back to school even though I wasn't feeling right. The other kids were very worried about me and, finally, the school rang Mum. She quickly discovered I was concussed, and she was very concerned about how the teachers had handled it. She felt the teachers showed a lack of compassion, and she had a strong feeling that if it had been the son of the principal, for instance, he would never have been left in the state I was.

She tried to raise it with the principal but he wasn't interested, so she took the case to the Department of Education and had it raised at a school committee meeting, demanding to know what the school policy was on treating injured children. The result was published in the school newsletter, and of course it showed that I had not been treated in accordance with school policy. Mum learned that direct confrontation doesn't always work, but there are other ways.

What really annoys me now — and annoyed Mum at the time — is that the schools were boxing me into this 'bad kid' role. I was doomed. If I wasn't a bad boy they were doing their best to make me a bad boy. One of the most humiliating things that happened was having the principal bribe me at the beginning of the term. I was asked to go to his office.

'What sort of things do you like?' he asked. 'Chocolate?'

'I like toy soldiers. War comics,' I replied.

'Well,' he said, 'if you can be a good boy we can give you those things.'

Looking back, I am pretty sure that some of what I was experiencing was just because I was Māori. But I also know that there was just as much prejudice towards me because of Mum being a solo parent: a solo parent on a benefit with children of mixed ethnicity. Those factors created a barrier in the community and made her and us kids vulnerable.

I remember one evening Mum had a friend visiting when an angry neighbour came pounding on the door at around 9 p.m. The neighbour was upset about something we kids had done — we'd left our bikes lying around or something like that — but she didn't just say her piece on the doorstep, she walked right into the house. I recall Mum's friend asking, 'How often does this happen? I bet it wouldn't happen if you had a man in the house.' And Mum said, 'Oh, it's just how they carry on.'

We had reason to be afraid of these kind of incursions, because on a summer's day, soon after we moved into our Pakūranga house, we experienced a violent home invasion. I was only four, and my brother was only a few days old and lying on his fleece in the lounge. My sister and I were with him when a man walked in off the street. He went straight past us and into the kitchen where Mum had been cutting up a watermelon.

'What are you doing in here?' we heard Mum say, and then he started beating her up. He beat her until she was bleeding, and he smashed watermelon over her, and then he picked up the knife. Luckily he didn't use it, but we — little kids standing in the doorway — were absolutely freaked out. We thought he was going to kill Mum. But instead he sat down to eat the watermelon, and someone — perhaps one of the neighbours — called the police. My sister and I saw the whole thing.

The police arrived, cuffed him and took him away. It turned out he was high on something. He wasn't a gangster, not a homeless guy, not a drunk; he was a member of a prominent Auckland family, and all the charges were eventually dropped.

We didn't know him at all. We were a random target of violence. Yet he came in and completely screwed up our lives. I'm sure I had post-traumatic stress disorder for several years, with nightmares and flashbacks. Now, of course, there's victim support but then there was nothing, and Mum was so busy recovering and managing the new baby that she didn't realise how affected I'd been. I couldn't stop thinking about the knife — this brown-handled knife with a long, skinny blade — and it wasn't until well into my teens that I could eat or even smell watermelon without being sick.

But something positive came out of that experience. One of the policemen was Māori — well, I thought he was. He had dark hair and dark eyes. A Māori guy in a uniform, saving us from a violent attacker. A hero. I didn't have many positive examples of Māori men in my life, but here was something to think about.

Another time a drunk neighbour came to the door and accused Mum of something, and I, a bit older by this time, stood in front of her to shield her. I was very protective of her. I thought, *This is not right*. I knew he wouldn't be here if my father was standing behind me. In fact, one time my uncle came round — one of my father's brothers — and he stood in front of this neighbour's house and said, 'If you bother this family again I'm going to give you a hiding.' That neighbour never caused any trouble again. So I know there's something about the protection a male can offer — and the protection doesn't have to be physical. It can be articulate and challenging. Mum did a lot of fighting in her life — standing up for us, standing up for herself, standing up for the community — but it's tiring, and not everyone is deterred by a single woman.

It seems to be a little bit harder doing it on your own.

//

Mum did so much for us, but one thing she couldn't give us was a sense of our Māori identity. We were very isolated, culturally. She was a Pākehā mother who didn't have the knowledge of the culture which, over time, would prove to be an important part of who we wanted to be.

I was an easy mark, being Māori in a largely non-Māori environment, and because of these expectations I became a stereotype. Quite quickly, I became the disinterested student sitting down the back of the class, not coming anywhere near my potential. This was where I was at.

Those experiences shaped who I am today.

CLOCKWISE FROM TOP:
A lovely photo of me and my older sister, Nikki. This was taken at a time in our lives when Mum was planning to leave Dad due to the same dysfunction that I see around me now. I see children who look just like we did, and I wonder — what if? // With Timaru family at a barbecue picnic around Christmas time. My mother created so many happy memories for us. // Me and my younger brother, Matt. I love this photo because it reminds me why we are so close today.

CLOCKWISE FROM TOP:
This photo (centre, third row) reminds me that I had a very happy childhood, which was safe and fun. All Kiwi kids deserve this chance. // Parihaka, 1990 (right). My time at Hato Petera College exposed me to an important, rich New Zealand history that I was not yet aware of. // I was proud to come home from Hato Petera to the suburbs of East Auckland. Not many kids in my neighbourhood had the chance to wear these formals.

PAKURANGA COLLEGE

PROGRESS REPORT

Name _Lance   O'Sullivan_
Christian Name   Surname

You have ability, but Form: _3 MS_   Date: _December, 1986._

You will never achieve
good results until Attendance: _1_ days absent out of _58_ days
H.P. PRINT
you start working
properly _J. Rogers_

SUBJECT	Attitude & Industry	Mark or Grade	COMMENTS
ENGLISH	2	47	Lance has appeared more willing to work this term. Quality still needs attention.
MATHEMATICS	3	64	Lance can achieve good marks in spite of inattention in class. *KM.*
SCIENCE	3	40	Lance has still a long way to go in achieving a satisfactory standard of work and concentration
SOCIAL STUDIES	3	50	Quantity of work governed by inclination rather than industry.
Core Music	3	34	Lance has done little to improve his standard.
Core Art	2	45	Lance enjoys his work. However he needs to take more care with finished work.
French	3	40	Lance needed to put much more effort into French this term. *um*
Economic Studies	2	60	When Lance can settle himself he is capable of good work particularly in Economics.
Physical Education	2	B/C	This mark could be 1.A.

Form Teacher's Comments:

Hopefully Lance will make more effort to reach his potential next year. _M.E. Marshall._

ATTITUDE AND INDUSTRY: 1. Excellent; 2. Satisfactory; 3. Should be better; 4. Unsatisfactory.
GRADES: A — 80%+; B — 65-79%; C — 45-64%; D — 20-44%; E — 0-19%.

The context of learning is so important. How did a change of environment result in such a dramatic change in outcome? It is clear that rigid models of service (in health or education) do not work for everyone.

HATO PETERA COLLEGE
WHUTUPAORO 1ST XV   1989
5TH PLACE NORTH HARBOUR SECONDARY SCHOOLS
SPONSORED BY SPACETIME INDUSTRIES

TOP: Kapa haka in Kaitāia, 1989 (centre, front row). Who would think that I would be centre stage again in this small country town, 20 years later?

BOTTOM: Being a reasonable rugby player (far left, front row) helped me settle in at Hato Petera. I loved the pride and history of the school.

CLOCKWISE FROM TOP LEFT: Proud Dad and Nana with Conor. The birth of your own child is a defining life moment. // Me, Conor and Dad. Whilst I had an estranged relationship with my father, I wanted our children to know who he was. // In my final year at medical school, getting ready to work at Middlemore Hospital. I was beginning to feel like a real doctor. // Brenny, me and Nana. My grandparents were good people. They were honest, sincere and kind; they taught me a lot about these important human qualities.

He aroha nui. My greatest love
and achievement has been to
have the whānau Tracy and
I have.

With Prime Minister John Key receiving the New Zealander of the Year Award, 2014. What turned out to be an amazing event, and an even more amazing 12 months that followed, almost did not happen — I had had thoughts of withdrawing from the process. I guess that age-old self-doubt was still lurking about. *Credit: The New Zealander of the Year Awards.*

Earning carbon credits in
the sun. Being involved
in multisport events has
helped me with fitness,
stress management and
health promotion.

That question again: Is it the student who is incapable, or is it the system that isn't capable of teaching the student? It's no different to my job as a doctor operating within the health system. Are Māori health statistics the result of a group of people who are incapable of being healthy, or a health system that's incapable of reaching their needs? I think the parallel is true, and so my early experiences in the education system resonate with my approach to delivering healthcare today.

I had a Māori teacher at my primary school. I was fascinated by him, really drawn to him: a Māori man, like my dad. It was a big thing for me. I had a romantic notion that Māori people would look at me and comfort me and take me under their wing — that's what I was seeking and hoping for. Yet he was particularly hard on me. One of the most hurtful things he did was to give me this wicked strap for being naughty. Usually when teachers gave you the strap on your hands they would place a book over the lower part of your arm, or hit from the side, so that the strap would only hurt your hand. But not this teacher. He did it right up my arm — bang, bang — and you could see the strap mark. I was really hurt by that, and I don't mean just physically.

A Māori teacher did this to me. I looked up to you, I thought you were good.

You often hear about these scenarios where people are harder on their own because they want them to do better, but I was too young to understand that. I don't even know whether that was the case.

Mum was furious and complained but I don't think it went anywhere. Isn't it bizarre to talk about this kind of thing today? Kids getting hit in the classroom. I know how I'd feel if any of my kids came home with strap marks on their arms. And yet I was lucky because the cane had already been stopped in that school (although it wasn't outlawed until 1990) — so it could have been worse.

Incidents like this were not good for my sense of cultural identity. Increasingly, my sense of culture was coming from this detachment.

//

Primary school hadn't worked out for me, but intermediate was better. I was still spending a lot of time in the principal's office and doing a few silly things, but in general it was a happier time. I had good friends and a great teacher — a young female teacher who I felt gave me a good chance. She tried to teach me how to count in Māori — in other words, she saw me, saw who I was. It's incredible the difference that can make. It's not money or having 10 cars up the drive — what can make the difference between keeping you in the system or losing you is just the one person who gives you a fair go. That's why I felt let down first in primary school and then in high school.

I'd say that if things had continued on the way they were at intermediate I would probably have been OK. I wasn't setting the world alight but I was mostly keeping out of trouble. But when I got to Pakuranga College, things went downhill again. It would be wrong to say that the teachers weren't giving me a fair go; I just think I had needs that the college couldn't help me with.

I was a teenage boy, with all the problems teenage boys can have around not listening, too much testosterone, too much aggression, not thinking rationally and all that. As far as the teachers went, I think that if you looked like you didn't want to learn you wouldn't get taught.

But I now believe that a situation like mine could be looked at through a different lens: a person who to one teacher appears like they don't want to learn is, to another teacher, a person who needs a different model of care, a different model of teaching. This is the understanding I bring to my medical practice today: we can't assume that everyone who isn't healthy doesn't want to be healthy. We just need to find a different way of communicating with them and inspiring them to be healthy.

So there I was, a young Māori person who had the potential to do great things with my life, but no one — myself included — was thinking that way. There were unique, cultural things about being Māori and if I'd had a chance to develop them they could have enhanced my ability to be a student, but at that time the school wasn't able to meet those needs.

I naturally gravitated to the small group of Māori kids who also went to Pakuranga College. I wanted to belong. I knew I was Māori, I was labelled as Māori, and yet I didn't know what it was to be Māori other than as a label and because of the colour of my skin. But of course these kids were the ones who got into trouble, and two of them were my cousins. They were real ratbags. I knew them well enough, having grown up with them off and on. I looked up to them. They were my role models. I was looking for my Māori identity, and they provided me with what seemed at the time like an answer.

I began getting into real strife.

On a school camp I got caught in the toilets with some kids who were smoking. We all got expelled from camp, and Mum had to come and get me. I thought it was unfair as I hated smoking and hadn't actually been doing it — but I shouldn't have felt too robbed. I was attracting this trouble because I was putting myself out there, hanging around with this group of kids. I wanted to be that type of person.

I didn't pay attention in class and was lippy to the teachers so was getting detention all the time. I got put into a special education class, the alternative stream — a class of kids who were mucking around. Basically, the teachers deemed that there was little hope for the kids in that class. No expectations of us — no good expectations, anyway.

Outside school I was in trouble as well. Stealing milk money, shoplifting at the supermarket. I was about 12 or 13 when I got caught. It's not rocket science why. Every day after school I'd come into the shop, choose a chocolate bar, wander up and down the aisles eating it, then hide the wrapper on the shelves. Obviously, when they were restocking they would have found the empty wrappers and thought, *Let's nab him. Let's see if this guy's stupid enough to come back.*

Sure enough, back I came. I ate my chocolate bar as usual and went to leave the shop, and no sooner was I past the checkout than the store detective grabbed me and said, 'Come with me.' I was taken to the manager's office and my mum was called.

'What's normal company procedure in the case of theft?' she asked.

'We'd normally call the police,' the manager told her.

'Do it,' she said.

The police arrived and again one of them was either a Māori or a Pasifika guy. They weren't impressed and told me my behaviour wasn't good enough. Then my mother arrived. She walked into the room, went straight past the cops, came up to me and went slap, slap, slap on my face.

She said, 'How could you bring me so much shame?'

Then she turned to the police and said, 'You deal with it.' And out she walked.

I was crying and honestly, the police were like, *What!* And this was years before Section 59 — the amendment to the Crimes Act that outlawed smacking children. That was an example of the shame Mum experienced every time I got into trouble. So by the time I got expelled in my second year of high school she was losing energy on the whole thing of getting her son to be good. Trying, trying, trying — but things kept getting worse.

She was so afraid I would end up following in my father's footsteps. Sometimes she'd lose her temper and say, 'You'll turn out like the bloody Watenes' — of course she would feel dreadful about it, but that's the kind of thing you say when your kid is being a ratbag and you're at your wits' end. The main reason she left Dad was because she knew she would survive one way or another, but that we kids wouldn't. She knew that living in that environment would predetermine how we would turn out.

But here I was turning out badly anyway.

Eventually, about halfway through my fourth-form year, Pakuranga College said they'd had enough of me. I was getting into trouble with my cousins, truanting and so on. The school had already suspended me a couple of times, so Mum asked to meet with the principal and deputy principal. They decided jointly that it was best I got out of that environment. It was agreed with Mum that I was going down the wrong track and that if I could be separated from those other kids I might have a better chance. They told Mum she needed to find another school, so I could make a fresh start.

She swung into action and approached Sacred Heart College, a large Catholic boys' college in the upmarket Auckland suburb of Glendowie. Mum pulled out all her big guns to try to get me into that school. Her uncle, Paul Scott, was a prominent Marist brother, really well known in the Catholic community, so she would have used his name. But despite that connection I guess they didn't like what they saw on my record. They were tentative. They said, 'Find somewhere else for Lance for the next three months. If he behaves himself, we'll take him next year.'

//

By this stage, Mum needed a break from me, and she thought it would help if I went to stay with her sister, who was married to a Māori guy of Ngāti Porou descent. They lived down in

Tīmaru on the family farm. My aunt was a bit reluctant — she had five boys of her own — but they agreed in the end. My nana was enlisted to get me into a college down there. She was unable to get me into the Catholic school, so she put on her Sunday best — gloves, the works — and we went for an interview at Timaru Boys' High. My grandparents were respected in the South Canterbury community, and her charm offensive worked. Timaru Boys' High agreed to take me for the remainder of the year.

Two months later I was expelled for fighting.

For weeks I had been feeling increasing animosity toward me from almost every boy in the school, due to my attitude. I had been training with a large, heavy grain bag hanging in the wool shed, with cloth bandages wrapped round my fists. I knew the day would come, and I think this preparation gave me a better chance on the day when a tough guy caught me out in a stairwell. The rest is history.

The plan had been that I would stay in Tīmaru until Mum came down with my sister and brother at Christmas. So I was stuck. I had to spend the next few weeks at home with my auntie. She was spewing. I wasn't getting on with my cousins, either — I felt they didn't want me there. I was behaving like an idiot, probably thinking *no one's going to tell me what to do*. It was a really unpleasant environment but those times helped me become a resilient person. Because, OK, you don't like me, and I can't do much about it. I'm getting into fights with you guys all the time, you're saying horrible things about me, but I have to get on anyway.

I learned how to enjoy my own company.

By the way, my relationship with those cousins now is awesome. We talk and email and they say how proud they are of what I've done, and I'm so proud they are part of my family. What happened back then was just a childhood moment, made worse by the state I was in and of course by the incredible guilt

I was feeling about letting Mum down, and Nana too, who'd gone in to bat for me with her gloves on.

Also, because I had been expelled from a second school, the deal was off with Sacred Heart. This was a big problem.

//

Things were not going well for me in my young life. I think that deep inside myself I was aware of the people around me having increasingly low expectations of my behaviour and my prospects. I had the same feeling I did when that principal tried to bribe me to be good. I felt really empty.

These experiences have had a profound effect on my beliefs as a doctor. What they spelled out to me was this: if you rob people of their self-belief, you deny them a bright future. I believed I couldn't be anything other than the naughty boy teachers perceived me to be. So I'll never turn a kid away and say he's a lost cause, or refuse to see a patient who others say is just trouble, aggressive and going to rip me off.

Mum had been aware for a while that it would be helpful if I knew who I was as a young Māori man. She had lived with my dad for long enough to understand that the Māori worldview is different to the Pākehā, and she knew it was the one thing she couldn't help me with. That understanding was partly behind her decision to send me down to stay with my aunt and uncle, and now she decided to reach out further.

She didn't consider sending me to live with my father — that way of life was not what she wanted me to experience. Neither did she approach his family. Some of her reluctance to ask my father's side of the family for help stemmed from the fact that she knew they were struggling with their own lives. She used to say to us: 'Don't go to other people with your problems. They've got enough of their own. You stay here and sort it out.' We children were her responsibility — not

Dad's, not our grandparents'. She knew she had to figure it out herself.

So she sat down and wrote to two Māori boarding schools, St Stephens and Hato Petera College. She told them of her difficulties as a Pākehā mother in providing the right kind of environment and knowledge for her son, and she requested help from them to give me what she couldn't. She explained that my father was absent and that we were largely alienated from my extended Māori family. Basically, she challenged them to step up. Hato Petera replied and agreed to interview us.

—

I WAS A KID AT THE CROSSROADS. I COULD GO EITHER WAY.

Back in Auckland, we drove over to the North Shore — after 10 years of biking, Mum at last had a car — to Hato Petera College and were interviewed by the principal, Toby Curtis, now Sir Toby Curtis, knighted for his services to Māori education. I wonder what he saw when he looked across his desk at me. I was probably a familiar enough sight to him. A young Māori lad, halfway down the wrong path. I didn't know then, but perhaps Sir Toby did, that I was a kid at the crossroads. I could go either way.

The statistics weren't in my favour: Māori were well behind Pākehā in their participation and their achievement in the education system. They had lower incomes, higher rates of unemployment, poorer health, and a much higher likelihood of getting convicted for a criminal offence. They were more likely to get into drugs and alcohol and tobacco, and to die as much as a decade or two younger than their Pākehā cohorts. The outlook for a young guy like me was, statistically speaking, bleak. I had no Māori language, no whakapapa, nothing to tell me who I was. I had a chip on my shoulder and a mounting anger towards an establishment that was already closing its door on me.

Toby Curtis looked at my mum. 'Yes,' he said. 'We'll take this boy on.'

//

Once a person has had a certain amount of success, it's easy for people to think: you guys are just too perfectly good to be real. They don't realise that behind the visible success is often a lot of other stuff: mistakes, hard times, maybe even historical realities that have made success hard to come by.

The work I'm doing today has been shaped by a whole lot of life experiences. But, fundamentally, what drives me in my work are the things that happened before I was born — my grandmother and grandfather feeding their children dog bones and dressing their children in flour sacks and breaking their backs in their garden because they had nothing. I want to bring them pride and mana, even though they've now passed on.

Those things have shaped what I do. But I also feel that because my path towards success wasn't smooth, my story could be very helpful for those who are challenged by their own circumstances. I want to inspire young people to not give up on their dreams.

I got knocked back at a number of points along the way. I didn't get into medical school the first time — but I went back and had another crack at it. And I'm proud that my achievements are not just in the world of medicine or the Māori world. I'm proud as a husband, a father, a son, of what I've been able to achieve in those areas of my life.

If someone had told me when I was a young person what I would have to go through to get to where I wanted to be, I would probably have said: I don't want to have any of that. I don't want to have the heartbreak of the son waiting for his father to turn up and he doesn't; I don't want the heartbreak of seeing the disappointment on my mother's face when she sees me getting kicked out of school again — her absolute sense of, *I'm at the end of my tether with this boy*. I would have baulked at the hard yards of medical school, and some of the demanding challenges of being a father and husband.

I wouldn't have chosen any of those things, but now I know that they've all helped shape who I am.

4 // THE FRONT ROW OF THE KAPA HAKA

On my first day at Hato Petera one of the Marist brothers, Brother Mark, approached me.

'Where are you from?' he asked kindly.

'I'm from Pakiranga,' I said in my best New Zild.

'Oh,' he said, 'Pah-koo-raanga.'

I could never say 'Pakiranga' again. I'd been corrected by a Pākehā man.

But he was right and that was really awesome. And, of course, when he asked where I was from he was really asking: Who are your people? What's your iwi? What's your waka? Your awa? Your maunga? I couldn't answer. I knew nothing about my whakapapa. I thought I might be Ngāpuhi — that was all I knew, and I wasn't even sure about that.

So here I was at my new school and I saw straight away it was going to be a baptism by fire. Until I got to Hato Petera my exposure to te reo had been limited to 'kia ora', and that one Pākehā teacher at intermediate who taught me how to count to 10 in Māori, and even then I only ever managed to get to five.

So, I could count to five and say kia ora. I now knew how

to say Pakūranga correctly — but beyond that I was ignorant. What's goodbye? What's goodnight? What's the Māori word for a shop or a lolly or a drink? All these things I take for granted now, but then, on the first day of my new life, I was all at sea.

My grandmother — my dad's mother — grew up in a traditional Māori family, free of alcohol and drugs and violence. She had a very strong relationship with her cultural heritage and would have been a fluent speaker of te reo. My grandfather grew up in the same sort of traditional environment and was also a fluent speaker. But he was heavily influenced by the Church of Latter-day Saints, and while the church does embrace Māori culture, the faith comes first and almost replaces the need for the marae and the culture.

The consequence for them was that as a result of religious belief, and the pressure of modern life — whether by conscious decision or just letting it slip away — the language and culture were abandoned. Dad, their son, couldn't speak a word of te reo. In one generation it was lost. It was only many years later that I came across a photo of my grandmother as a very young woman, in full Māori dress, and learned she'd been part of a concert party that travelled to England, singing waiata and performing kapa haka. By the time I came along, there was no visible trace of any of that background, and Dad knew nothing about it.

You often hear about families who made a decision not to speak Māori because 'you need English so you can get ahead in this world'. Our old people talk about that all the time. They stopped their children learning Māori because of that idea. I suspect that was part of the reason my father never learned te reo — his parents would have said, 'Look, it's best you don't learn our language. If we try to teach you both you'll get confused.'

As a young boy I looked up to my father and wanted to be like him. I knew he was Māori, and thought that could bring us together:

I want to know who I am as a Māori because that will bring me closer to him.

Up until my young adulthood I had a real sensitivity about not being authentic and legitimate. It bit hard into my self-esteem. Quite reasonably so, in my mind — I was always being made to feel that I didn't fit in. At Hato Petera there were guys fairer than me, yet I was called the white boy: my nose not flat enough, my skin and eyes not dark enough.

Even now people will say to me: 'You don't look Māori, you don't sound Māori. You look Italian or European.' How rude is that? They're actually telling me what I should look like. The reality is we're such a melting pot of people now. But as a young man this all contributed to my sense of uncertainty and confusion. I didn't look the part and I didn't know where I was from.

—

MY GRANDMOTHER GREW UP IN A TRADITIONAL MĀORI FAMILY, FREE OF ALCOHOL AND DRUGS AND VIOLENCE.

And now I was about to be immersed in tikanga Māori.

I was a long way behind the other boys my age. I was thrust into my new life at form five, which today we call year 11. All the other students had already had two years of language, two years of kapa haka. And most of them looked more Māori than me. I seemed to be behind the eight-ball on everything.

By that stage, Dad had gone to live in Australia and I hardly ever saw him. However, he did turn up at the school once or twice and that was very meaningful for me because he's really dark and I could say to everyone, 'See! I told you I was a Māori!'

It was confirmation: *I'm not a fraud; I've got a right to be here.*

//

At a Hato Petera gala dinner in 2014, to celebrate the knighthood of former principal Sir Toby Curtis and my being named New Zealander of the Year, Sir Toby joked that he'd agreed to let me into the college because I had strong shoulders and he thought I'd be good at rugby.

'No,' I said, 'I'm sure you saw the calibre of the person, given that I'd just been expelled from two colleges and had a great big chip on my shoulder.'

At the interview — Mum all dressed up, of course — I probably sat there and went, 'Yip, yip, nah'. But, of course, Sir Toby had seen it all before. It was not unusual for kids at Hato Petera to come from really rough backgrounds. I think about a third of the kids were under social welfare care at the time and were very troubled, so I wasn't anything new. Others were prospective gang members. I think if some of the kids weren't there they'd have been in juvenile detention.

Hato Petera College is now 87 years old and has produced some of the greatest Māori minds in the country. Sir Ranginui Walker, Sir Toby Curtis, Ralph Hotere, Arapeta Tahana, Jamie Tuuta, Oscar Nathan — a real variety of people have come out of the school. Someone said to me once that if you look in the boardrooms around the country, Māori from Hato Petera and other boarding schools are there.

Life at Hato Petera was very structured. We got up early, went to classes, had lunch in the dining room, went back to school. After school we had a bit of free time before we had to do clean-up, then we had dinner and then chapel and then study and then bed. It was rigid.

There was a hierarchy in our routine which I had never experienced before — the hierarchy of authority. The brothers provided this formal overseeing and then there were the senior students. You did as you were told by the senior students and if you didn't you got a kick up the backside. You respected their authority and it wasn't just their physical mana. They had earned their position and they displayed and demonstrated their right to tell you what to do.

I was initially really lonely. I tried to run away once, soon after I first arrived. I got as far as the Harbour Bridge but of course I couldn't get over it.

That chip on my shoulder didn't make things easy; I thought the world owed me a lot. I had 14 years of wanting to have a father and I didn't have one. I wanted to have the things that other kids had. I was sick of teachers saying I was bad all the time when I didn't feel I was always bad. I was annoyed about that, and annoyed about feeling shitty everywhere I went. I was still smarting from when a carload of hoons had driven very slowly past me outside the Pakūranga supermarket and thrown a can of fizzy drink at me and shouted that I was a nigger. Worst of all, I believed that whatever I did, I was likely to fail.

There had been some hard things in my life, and I certainly had many challenges ahead of me — personal challenges, professional challenges — but what I can say now is this: the challenging times are sent to give you a bit of steel in your backbone. One way or another, they shape you.

Being at that school was a real wake-up call. I saw there were a lot of kids worse off and far tougher than me. I saw I didn't need to have a chip on my shoulder. I did have some real, immediate problems, though, like how to protect myself.

Boys' boarding schools are notoriously tough environments, and I got a few hidings — dragged down to the swimming pool area late one night and slapped around, more to humiliate than to cause physical harm. One was funny in retrospect — on a kapa haka trip I'd had to take off my piupiu and lend it to another performer, so I grabbed a nearby pair of trousers. A few minutes later, a big, scary guy, one of the Black Power prospects, came up to me.

'Hey, those are my pants. You're gonna effin' get it.'

I gave him his pants back, but I knew that wasn't the end of it and, sure enough, three nights later as I was walking home from kapa haka practice a fist came out of the dark and got me in the side of the face, giving me a massive black eye. I saw stars.

When these things happen at boarding school, the staff don't really get involved. The brothers probably thought I deserved it. I was only new but maybe I was walking around as if I was the man. I probably thought I was more of the man than I was. Maybe I was cocky. Whatever it was, my behaviour was causing me some challenges and I had to work out if I was going to keep going as I was, or try to change the way I was behaving. Some boys who started at the same time as me didn't last and left the school, but I quickly decided I would stick it out.

Even though it was lonely at first, I was used to being on my own. I'd been unpopular at school for the past three years, and I'd also just been in Tīmaru at a school where no one liked me, and then with my cousins who didn't like me either. I'd become quite secure in my own company, and that was lucky because for the first six months at Hato Petera I had no friends.

I saw guys who turned up after me fitting in better, being popular straight away. That sucks, eh! On a Friday night when everyone else was getting into groups for ice cream and soft drinks I was on my own. If someone invited me to join them, that was the highlight of my week. I was so isolated that sometimes I'd hang out with young kids, third formers, which was a big step down for a fifth former.

I never chased popularity. I just let people know, *This is who I am*, and I didn't rush into building friendships that weren't going to last. And in the end, of course, I did find friends — and those friendships have been lifelong.

Unlike many of the other guys, I drew my friends from across the spectrum. Maybe because of all that loneliness I knew myself well enough to figure out what I needed and wanted. Some guys I became friends with had good study habits. I made friends with guys who were clean and looked after their appearance. Other guys went to the gym and they liked to keep fit. And others were just good fun and liked to have parties. So I had all these groups of friends, and they respected me for being different from them. My friends who were really good at studying weren't into sport or going to the gym, so I'd study with them but then go and play a really good game of rugby. But then the guys who played rugby didn't want to study. They wanted to party all the time and smoke dope. But they were accepting of the fact that I didn't want to smoke dope. I partied heaps with them, but then I'd be like, 'Hey look, I've got to study.'

I really liked being someone who set clear boundaries and had clear ideas of who I was. They'd often mock me — 'Oh you're going off to eat your muesli in the kitchen again on your own' — because even back then I had these finnicky tastes, but I was trying to get ready for the day.

And these friends were the guys who turned up to support me when I won New Zealander of the Year — the same ones I met way back then as a 15-year-old, and we have stood by each other for nearly 30 years. People like Oscar Nathan, who went on to become an NZIM Young Executive of the Year; Valance Smith, a real fun guy who everyone liked; the rugby guys who everyone looked up to; Tawhai Waititi, the East Coast bushman; Hilton Harris, the smooth-talking Hokianga lad; Jason King and Reweti Smith, the kapa haka boys.

Sometimes we don't see each other for years, but when we do it's like it was yesterday. *You and I lived together for three years; we know each other as close as brothers.* I've been really fortunate because my kids have grown up with all these guys they rightly call uncle, and in turn my family has seen their kids grow up and the kids call each other cousin.

So while I had to work really hard to conform in the beginning, I quickly realised I was in the right place — exactly where I needed to be. For the first time in my life I was surrounded by positive male role models, many of them Māori. The principal and senior teachers were Māori. All the boys were Māori, and I was thrown into the culture.

//

The first kapa haka practice. I loved it, but every time I was meant to be standing up I'd be down on my knees and every time everyone else was down on their knees I was standing up.

Whenever there was a public performance I'd get embarrassed because I was always behind, but I look back on it and laugh. I was 15 and just beginning to learn, but now our kids are so culturally strong, even at seven. And that's within one generation. I'm really proud of what I've achieved — bringing in all the values from my grandparents' heritage, my mother's spirit and self-respect, and the lessons that I've learned myself. The language, the tikanga were lost in my grandparents' generation, but they weren't lost forever. The new generation can be strong and proud Māori who know their language and their culture.

As a young boy I didn't have a very close relationship with my grandmother, my father's mother. She struggled a lot in her life and Mum didn't like to impose us on her. Dad took me to see her a few times, but I never had the opportunity to spend as much time with her as I did with my mother's family. But we loved each other dearly and when she saw me pursuing the culture she was delighted. In my first year at Hato Petera we went on a school trip to Thames and Paeroa and we stayed on the Matai Whetu marae, just behind my grandmother's house. She came to watch one of our kapa haka performances, and she gave me what is probably my most sacred taonga, a large whalebone manaia. It was funny because here I was, this young guy who didn't know anything about what he was doing, yet I was wearing this really prestigious taonga and it was flying all over the place as I tried my best to keep up with the other performers. I was probably right at the back, which is where they put all the newbies, but I was in heaven. And from then on my relationship with my nana became really strong.

By the time I left Hato Petera I had made it into the front row of the kapa haka.

//

The hangover from my experiences at primary, intermediate and early secondary school was that I really didn't think I was capable of succeeding at school. That hangover lasted a long time. But what Hato Petera did for me, among other things, was give my confidence a boost. At my last year at school I won heaps of awards: for science, biology, English, mathematics, swimming, athletics, rugby. I pretty much just stayed up on stage. Not bad for a boy who had looked set for failure, as my mother said proudly.

At Hato Petera I had really passionate teachers, but it was a small school and had many focuses apart from just academic. So even though I had become very successful in that context, I was a big fish in a small pond and I think, deep down inside, I knew that. I still had doubts about my ability to compete against kids from schools where there were 2000 students and they were turning out Cambridge scholars.

I certainly had never considered that I could go to university. You know what — I had about 80 cousins and not one single one had ever gone on to university, and neither had anyone from all the generations before. However, towards the end of seventh form, my teachers started saying, 'You could consider these options: law, teaching, medicine . . .' And I was like, *Really?* No one in my family was a doctor. I had never known anyone who was a doctor. But then it just started hitting home that being a doctor was a possibility.

It occurred to me that medicine was a vehicle by which I could make a contribution, something that I had begun to think I was capable of. I felt I was indebted to my people — yes, I had begun thinking in those terms: *my people*. And, in fact, this is something I often say — that what I'm doing today is exactly why, way back then, I went to medical school: to make a contribution to a community of people who need it.

I was young, but I already intuitively understood the broad truths of my people's situation. It wasn't hard to see. My grandmother was very poor and was already ill with diabetes — the disease that would kill her prematurely, as it does so many Māori.

I was seeing the widespread dispossession, and the disenfranchised looks on my people's faces. I saw it at family events, in the schools I went to, and I read about it. I was becoming politically aware of the issues, of land and history, the lack of wellbeing as a whole. Of course at that age I wasn't thinking, 'I'm going to help reduce rheumatic fever. I'm going to help reduce diabetes complications. I'm going to help reduce smoking rates. I'm going to help increase physical activity among Māori.' I didn't know the actual nuts and bolts, but I wanted to be a leader for my people, and I just felt that if I was a doctor I could help.

So I applied for medical school. I was young and more confident than I'd ever been. I went along with my friend Oscar Nathan for support, and we blew them away with our mihi and waiata — we were the cultural kings of the interviewing process. And they said I was exactly what they wanted: 'If you can get a B bursary, you're in.'

But when the Bursary results came back I'd failed. I hadn't managed to get 50 per cent in any of my five subjects. I hadn't got into medical school. The bubble burst.

I'm not smart.

I was runner-up Dux of Hato Petera, but it had only 250 kids and it wasn't exactly the academic stronghold of the country. Now I could see that 'smart' was only a measure of relativity. And the little nagging doubt, the thing that sat inside me whispering, *This is not true, this is not going to last*, turned out to be right after all.

I had passionate teachers, but was it because I didn't have the teachers I needed that I didn't get a bursary, or was it because I didn't have the goods? I had worked hard for the exams. Maybe I'd been learning the wrong things? No one in my year at Hato Petera passed Bursary.

Yet Oscar went on to become Young Executive of the Year and is currently the general manager of Destination Rotorua Marketing, and out of our seventh-form year of 20, there have been three or four PhDs, and one doctor. So I don't know what that means, except that school results are not the absolute indicator of success in life.

5 // WHAKAPAPA

E tū pakari ana ahau kei mua i a koutou i ngā
    waewae e rua.
Tētahi taha nō Hauraki whenua, nō *Tainui* waka,
    nō Ngāti Maru te iwi.
Tētahi taha nō Te Tai Tokerau, nō *Ngā-toki-mata-*
    whao-rua, nō Ngāpuhi, me Te Rarawa.

I stand strong in your presence on two feet.
On one side I am from the Hauraki nation, from the
    Tainui waka, from the Ngāti Maru tribe.
On one side I am from the Northland confederation,
    from the *Ngā-toki-mata-whao-rua* waka, from the
    Ngāpuhi and Te Rarawa tribes.

When I was at Hato Petera, and someone asked me who I was
and where I was from, it was embarrassing to not know the
answer. It was my moment of realisation — that I didn't know
who I was as a Māori. That was what was missing in my life.
Learning who I was as a Māori was the single most important

thing that turned my life around. Learning the language and culture filled me with strength. But it wasn't enough.

I needed to find out who I was before I was born. I needed to discover my whakapapa. Sir Āpirana Ngata, the great reformer and politician of the late nineteenth and early twentieth centuries, described whakapapa as 'the process of laying one thing upon another' — ancestral connections, and also relationship to landscape. Whakapapa connects us to the past, but also to the present as it establishes a network of living connections.

For instance, if I go to a marae on the East Coast it's really meaningful if I know enough about my own whakapapa and enough about their history so I can make a connection. My knowledge and research allows me to identify that 200 years ago an ancestor from my area married someone from your area, and that the name of our tupuna is carried in that rocky headland just out there. I can stand there as one of you, and pay my respects. That is very important. It enhances the prestige of the group far beyond just being a hospitable host for the night. This is what the best orators do. Their kōrero will always include their own relevance to the people they're talking to.

So whakapapa is not just about an individual's lineage, but the entire sense of connectedness it provides, through time and across geography. When you give your whakapapa you say, this is my marae, this is my river, this is my mountain. I have been to all my mountains and walked up them with Tracy and the kids, so that rather than just talking about these places we know them — we've walked the marae and the mountain and the whenua we talk about.

I use this in my practice all the time. I always ask my patients who they are and where they come from. It makes them feel a bit more valued beyond just being a number.

Learning my whakapapa was part of building a life for myself that was strongly linked to a wider extended family and, later, for the ideal family that I wanted to create with Tracy, where our children would be secure in their identity.

But so much knowledge had been lost. I had become close to my grandmother — my father's mother, Maggie Ruka — but when she died in my first year of medical school of diabetes complications, she took all the deep historical knowledge of the family with her. She had told Mum she had knowledge to pass on to me but that I was too young for some of it, and that's hard to know: that she had the knowledge, she wanted to give it to me, but she was waiting for the right time. She left it too late. So I had to go looking.

//

I was in my thirties when I began researching in earnest. I talked to elders, piecing together bits of information. I did a lot on my computer at night, using the Mormon Church's online genealogy records, and at lunchtimes I popped into the Māori Land Court to work in their archives. Land Court records are a very rich resource for whakapapa because when the hearings were taking place, in the late nineteenth century, Māori had to prove their ownership of the land through whakapapa, often going back 200 years or more, and it was all put down in writing.

Stories emerged from that process, about battles fought, land taken or gifted. Personalities emerged, like my grandmother's ancestor Tarutaru, who was there at the great battle in the Kaipara region when Te Rarawa got its name. Tarutaru was a ferocious fighter who never stepped backwards and was so terrifying to look upon that his enemies' courage would fail them.

My grandmother Maggie Ruka was from Ngāpuhi, Ngāti Hau and Te Rarawa. She came from Whakapara, a small Māori settlement north of Hikurangi, and often travelled from there to visit her mother's whānau at Pukepoto, between Kaitāia and Ahipara. Her great-great-great-grandfather was Eru Patuone, a renowned Ngāpuhi identity who was present at the signing of the Treaty of Waitangi, where he persuaded a number of chiefs to sign the document. His grave is on Mount Victoria in Auckland's Devonport.

My grandfather Mita Pirimona Watene was from Ngāti Maru of Hauraki. His whakapapa begins in Hawaiki with the ancestor Rongokako, who was part of the great migration aboard the *Tainui* waka to Aotearoa and the Waikato region. After 16 generations, my ancestor Marutūāhu left the Waikato and moved to Hauraki, where my grandfather was born about 13 generations later.

It was a very exciting time for me as I put my family's history together. I even made a connection with my father, which is something I'm proud of. I asked him to show me the caves in the hills above my grandparents' old homestead back in Kōpū. It's where all our tūpuna are buried, so it is a sacred area for our tribe. He had been taken by his father, and now he took me, and I in turn can take my sons. That is very important to me.

I GAVE MY FAMILY BACK ITS IDENTITY.

There was some history there, too, because in 1823 Hōne Heke came down to Hauraki and slaughtered many people. One of our tūpuna, a young teenage boy, had the job, along with the whānau, to take the bodies of the massacre victims and, I believe, inter them in the caves, which are like crevices in the walls of the mountainside. So they are a very tapu site.

Some people say they are so sacred you shouldn't visit them, yet I felt very comfortable and peaceful up there. And Dad is now buried in the urupā where the massacre took place.

My research over seven or eight months culminated in my writing a slim book, *Te Whanau Watene*, which is like a family album, going right back to Rangi and Papa. Through it, I gave my family back its identity.

And, in November 2005, at Matai Whetu marae in Thames, near the homestead where my father and his brothers and sisters grew up, we had the inaugural Watene whānau hui, where the Watenes came together for the first time to explore and discover our whakapapa. Organising the hui required quite a bit of leadership because life is tough for a lot of people and they just want to get on with it. But I was determined, and it was worthwhile. We had over 90 people attending, eight of whom were the children of Maggie and Mita, including my father Eddy.

//

In 2014 Tracy and I were invited to Tainui, to the Māori King's Matariki celebration dinner. I was proud to stand up and connect myself to that gathering through my whakapapa:

'E tū pakari ana ahau kei mua i a koutou i ngā waewae e rua. Tētahi taha nō Hauraki whenua, nō *Tainui* waka, nō Ngāti Maru te iwi.' I'm standing under the auspices of the *Tainui* waka because this is my father's side, my grandfather's side.

'Tētahi taha nō Te Tai Tokerau, nō *Ngā-toki-mata-whao-rua*, nō Ngāpuhi, me Te Rarawa.' When I stand on this leg, I'm standing under the auspices of Ngāpuhi confederation because this is my grandmother's side.

What it means is that this person standing here before you today stands on two legs. I need both of these legs to stand strong and true.

I was essentially saying to that Tainui gathering, 'Kia ora, I'm one of you; I'm one of yours.' It puts people at ease. And I got this lovely response from the audience and that was neat. I will always try to find a connection with the people I'm addressing. This is not about celebrating me as the speaker — it's about the speaker celebrating his connection to the audience. It enhances the mana of the audience for a link to be made in this way. I see this with my patients in my medical practice too: once we have established that we have something in common, some communality, there is a revelation. We are connected. We are relevant to each other.

I WILL ALWAYS TRY TO FIND A CONNECTION WITH THE PEOPLE I'M ADDRESSING. THIS IS NOT ABOUT CELEBRATING ME AS THE SPEAKER — IT'S ABOUT THE SPEAKER CELEBRATING HIS CONNECTION TO THE AUDIENCE.

If it's a mainstream audience I'm talking to I'll say, on this side I belong to my mother and that's my Irish whakapapa. On the other side I belong to my father and that's my Māori lineage.

In belonging to these different tribes, there is no confusion or sense of conflict for me. I belong to Ngāpuhi, Tainui, Te Rarawa, Ngāti Hau and Ngāti Maru and Ngāti Pākehā, and I think it's a huge bonus to have strong connections to each of these different communities. At certain times it's right to step forward and say, I live in Muriwhenua, I live in Kaitāia, and it's appropriate that I celebrate my connections to the local iwi, Te Rarawa.

But at other times it's appropriate to celebrate my connection to my grandfather's side. For instance, I've been asked to be a patron for a Māori language revitalisation strategy in Hauraki. It's a huge honour, and I said to the person who asked me, 'This is wonderful because I'm up here [in Kaitāia] doing work on my grandmother's side, but I thank you for the opportunity to go back to Hauraki and play a leadership role there, too.'

//

When I was about 17 I went through a time of thinking that I needed to change my name to reflect my Māori identity. As it happened, the name on my birth certificate was already Lance Watene, although I had always been known as Lance O'Sullivan. I decided I now wanted to be known as Lance Watene. I wanted the world to know my connection to the Watene family of Thames. People said I didn't look Māori, and my non-Māori name didn't help. Watene would make me more outwardly Māori.

However, my mum got really upset. She said I had been raised all these years as Lance O'Sullivan. She had brought me up. After a lot of thought, I ended up changing my name by deed poll to Lance O'Sullivan.

I am who I am. If people are going to know me, it's got to be through my actions. It's got to be through the things I actually achieve in my community.

I am proud of my lineage on both sides — Māori and Pākehā. I am proud of the work I did with my family's whakapapa. It's given our family something that, if I was 13 again and the whakapapa was put in my hands, would make a big difference.

It makes a big difference to me now.

WHĀIA TE ITI KAHURANGI KI TE TUOHU KOE ME HE MAUNGA TEITEI

//

AIM FOR THE HIGHEST CLOUD SO THAT IF YOU MISS IT, YOU WILL HIT A LOFTY MOUNTAIN

PART 2 //

—

BUILDING A
FAMILY AND
A CAREER

6 // THURSDAY NIGHT DOLLAR DRINKS

L ife is wonderful for me today. The future is so bright. I feel I'm able to do a whole lot of really good things and people recognise that. The opportunities opening up for me are amazing. And all this — this happy feeling of possibility — was exactly how I felt in my final year of college.

Now, if I imagine losing everything I have — my licence to practise medicine, my job, my family, my credibility and respect — well, it would be a catastrophe. If you can imagine that kind of loss, you can imagine how terrible it was for me when I failed Bursary and didn't get into medical school. The path I was on suddenly ran out and I was lost.

'Go and do a BSc,' the medical school said to me, 'and we'll see how things go.'

So I enrolled at the University of Auckland. I'd been in a brotherhood of 250 Māori kids, hearing our language, singing our songs. In the end I'd loved boarding school so much I didn't want to come home when we had free weekends. My world had become very small — no bigger than the kura. Now I was in an anonymous crowd of 20,000 students. All my mates had gone to the University of Waikato and I was completely isolated. I hated it. I couldn't cope.

I had a little Yamaha 125 that I used to ride from Pakūranga, where I was living again with my mother, and as I drove through Mission Bay and along the waterfront towards the university I'd be crying.

I hate this; I'm a failure. I failed and I don't know why I'm pursuing this.

About four months into the year, I quit.

I didn't know what I was going to do, so I enrolled on the dole. I used to go down to Mission Bay on a Thursday, collect my dole, get a *Trade and Exchange*, get a malt milkshake, read the *Trade and Exchange* to see if there were any jobs, go home, and wait for the next night out with the boys, or the next chance to play football. I was doing nothing. My life was empty. I had enough to keep me busy, doing little things for Mum, but it was a massive change from what I thought I'd be doing. I honestly thought I'd go straight to medical school from college — college where I was hugely successful and popular and everything was laid out.

I was cushioned by the fact that I was young and as long as I could have fun, play a bit of sport, I could keep my spirits up. But I knew this wasn't somewhere I wanted to be forever. After a while I thought, *Every Thursday is the same as the last.*

So after about six months, I got a job — probably because Mum was sick of me hanging around at home. I was paying her rent, of course, but I knew she was worried and disappointed about what was happening with me. When I was in seventh form she had really celebrated the success I had. She had made herself a part of it — like she does now — getting to know my friends, being involved as a parent in the school, making amazing meals for us after our rugby matches. But now I noticed her flatness around me.

So I went and got a cadetship at the New Zealand Customs Department. *I won't worry about medicine*, I thought. *I'll just look at a career as a customs officer.*

And to begin with, I liked it. I enjoyed the enforcement side of it, and the excitement around catching people bringing in the wrong stuff. There were career possibilities. However, conforming to the rules and rigours of government departments turned out to be challenging for me. I'd envisaged an exciting medical career, but here I was in an office much of the time doing menial tasks, searching for files in the filing room, stamping the five carbon copies on import licences. Stamp, stamp, stamp, the stamper automatically turning over because it was set for five copies. There would be a table of about six or eight of us, and we'd all be stamping away. When we finished one we'd put it in a pile and reach for the next one. I can remember the number on the licence — AKS 137 — at the moment I realised, *I don't want to do this with my life. I honestly think I can do more.*

Then I met Tracy. I was out on the town, in a bar with some mates — Thursday night dollar drinks — when I saw her. A beautiful Māori woman. I asked her to dance and she said no. *Oh, OK.* I was pretty brave, but that would knock anybody. Then a couple of weeks later I met her again and this time she said yes.

//

As it turned out, Tracy had also grown up in East Auckland. She even went to the same secondary school — Pakuranga College — but because I was two years younger than her she'd never noticed me. She grew up with her Pākehā mum and Māori dad and three older sisters in a very different kind of household to mine.

Her dad, who is Te Arawa, had been sales manager for a

multinational medical supplies company and they'd lived in San Francisco for two years when Tracy was young. When they came back to New Zealand her parents set up their own business, importing medical laboratory equipment and supplies. So they were a family with lots of connections to the medical world. One of Tracy's sisters is a GP and had been the youngest graduate at medical school; and Tracy herself began training as a nurse as soon as she left school at the end of the sixth form.

She graduated at 19 and was still too young to be registered as a nurse, so she waitressed at Valentine's for three months while she waited for her twentieth birthday the following January. Once registered, she got a job at Auckland Hospital, where she was still working when I met her about two years later.

Tracy chose nursing partly because she knew it was a good career if you wanted to have a family one day — but she had no thoughts of beginning a family right then. She and a friend had been saving hard and booked their one-way tickets to London. They were also going on a 30-day Contiki tour around Europe and the Greek islands. Tracy had her British nursing registration, and lots of money saved. It was all sorted.

That suited me. Neither of us was looking for a long-term relationship. We had a fantastic couple of months that summer, including hitchhiking down to Tīmaru to see my grandparents. It was lots of fun, but we both knew it wasn't going to last because Tracy was leaving. Then two weeks before she was to leave New Zealand, she discovered she was pregnant.

Having a termination was out of the question for Tracy, not because of any religious reasons, but simply because she felt this new life inside her was her responsibility. Neither could she any longer imagine heading overseas. Being on a bus for a month with a whole bunch of 20-year-olds who would all be drinking had seemed like heaps of fun, but it didn't any more. She knew she might get morning sickness and would probably be tired. Her trip was off.

It was a shock for both of us. Tracy sat down with me and Mum and she said, 'Look, I have a career. I already have my qualification. I have a supportive family. I can do this on my own and I don't expect you to do it with me. I don't expect us to get married.' She knew I was only young, and that was her gift to me.

Tracy also assured Mum: 'Whatever happens between Lance and me, you will always have a relationship with this child as its grandmother.'

But I'd been brought up by a solo mother, and I wasn't about to let that happen to a child of mine. We made the decision that we'd do it together. We would keep this baby and I would be a good father to it.

And that's how it happened. We didn't live together until Conor was born, but at that point I moved in with them, into a self-contained flat at Tracy's parents' house, and we began our great journey together.

One of the things that attracted me to Tracy was her Māori background. Of course she's got all her other amazing personal qualities as well, but I need to acknowledge that her being Māori was really important to me and I wanted to continue on the pathway of living a Māori life with a Māori family.

Tracy has a huge extended family in Rotorua. At that time her Pākehā grandfather and Te Arawa grandmother were still alive and she was very close to them. She'd spent all her school holidays down there and absolutely loved it. When Conor was born he became her grandmother's one hundred and fifty-fifth mokopuna, which includes grandchildren and great-grandchildren, and there were many more before she died at 94.

Despite that family, though, Tracy had grown up in a middle-class, largely Pākehā area and been to a middle-class Pākehā school where there were hardly any Māori kids. As a child she didn't notice any overt disapproval of her for being

Māori, although as an adult there are a few things she looks back on and wonders about — some of her friends' parents were not keen on her being mates with their children, for instance. So when she was with certain friends she would play down being Māori. Like me, she didn't know how to pronounce Māori words properly. She just considered herself 'a New Zealander'.

BEING MĀORI WAS REALLY IMPORTANT TO ME AND I WANTED TO CONTINUE ON THE PATHWAY OF LIVING A MĀORI LIFE WITH A MĀORI FAMILY.

Her father made some efforts to bring Māori culture into their daily lives. He wrote out all the words for 'Pōkarekare Ana' on a big piece of paper and he made his kids sing it as he played the guitar. Yet, Tracy says, she got the message that there was a negative connotation to being Māori. From how people talked, the casual things they'd say — *Māori are lazy, Māori don't want to work*. Tracy's father, Ken Macfarlane, was a successful businessman and one of her uncles, Angus Macfarlane, is a professor at Canterbury University (and both graduated from Hato Petera College). While she had this real affinity with her whānau in Rotorua, and loved the parties where they'd break out the guitars and everyone would sing, she hadn't really thought about being Māori, and learning the language and culture.

Tracy comes from a very stable family with a mother and father who have complete dedication and love for their children and, now, their grandchildren, and they promote the importance of whānau both in the immediate family and the extended family. What I have witnessed in my father-in-law is what I would like to feel that I could achieve, where the grandchildren love him and respect him, as do his children and their partners.

So, with Tracy, I knew I could offer our kids the kind of rich family connection that hadn't yet been possible in my own Māori family. I could live a lot of what I would have hoped for myself and my kids through her. And she became a willing partner in our shared journey as young Māori determined to become strong in our culture and our values, and to work for the betterment of our people.

We come from different walks of life, with very different backgrounds, but I think we complement each other heaps. Tracy gave me a life which was a perfect family: the husband, the wife, the kids. It was perfect, and it is perfect.

//

No one puts you in a class and teaches you how to be a good father. No one recognises that sons brought up by mothers might struggle to even know what good fathering is. It's by chance that a good male teacher might come into their lives; and we leave it to chance that these young boys will be good fathers. Some are, some aren't.

I was excited about fatherhood. I thought it was an opportunity to redeem that part of my life. I so badly wanted to be everything I had missed out on with my own father.

When Tracy became pregnant with Conor, it was a surprise. A big surprise. I was only 20, and Tracy was 21, and we'd been together only three months. We certainly weren't secure in our relationship, but neither of us ever considered the possibility of not having this baby.

Like other men who missed out on having a good father, I was so desperate not to be like my father that I strove to overachieve. I still do. I want to do more than what an average father does. So I set the bar high. Of course sometimes I don't always reach that level. Sometimes I lose it and get angry. I disappoint myself, but I have never lost that strong, urgent desire to do a really good job of being a father.

Every parent understands the awesomeness of birth. *Oh my gosh, what just happened?* I went from being the son of my mother and father, to being the father of our son. And I loved it. And pretty soon we had Te Miringa, then Nina, then Te Hira, Wairua, Taikehu and Lance. Tracy and I have been together for 23 years and we have seven children — five sons and two daughters. We thought, this is fun, we do a good job, we're producing wonderful, beautiful Māori kids. I have a real sense of pride about this. Hey, we've got an opportunity to stamp our mark on the world through our kids.

So my message to other young men who have missed out on being fathered is this: you don't have to also miss out on being a good father to your own children. If you look around carefully you will find someone in your life, in your community, who can demonstrate to you how to be a good father, a good husband and a good man. You just have to look more carefully, more consciously, than if that role model had been on your own doorstep all along.

Some aspects of parenting won't come naturally to us and we may not have all the answers, but if — like me — you passionately want to be a good father, you will keep trying. When things go wrong, acknowledge this to yourself, remembering that you either didn't have a role model who helped or one who was not so flash. Don't beat yourself up — but do go out of your way to find positive people to be around. If you spend time with good people, that is what will become normal for you, and your own behaviour.

//

I never stopped trying to reach out to my dad. I was always giving him the opportunity to be the father I wanted him to be.

Something I struggled with as a parent was that my temper was very short. Looking after kids takes patience and tolerance and sometimes those qualities are in short supply. Now and then I'd get really frustrated and volatile with the demands of parenthood, and I'd never learned how to deal with those feelings in any way other than through anger. You know, that *rrrrrr* feeling, when your child won't do what you want them to do — how do you deal with that?

One time I smacked Conor, quite a hard smack, the kind that these days would land you in court, and I felt really bad about it. This might seem strange, but my instinct was to ring my dad. When he picked up the phone, I said, 'I'm really upset, Dad. I hit Conor and I'm not happy about it.'

'You'll be right,' he said. 'You had worse than that. Didn't do you any harm.'

It was so gut-wrenching to hear that sort of advice. I wanted him to say, 'OK, let's talk about it. You were really stressed out, and it's hard being a father. Let's look at some other ways of dealing with your feelings.'

I'd sometimes ring him when I was upset; maybe a child had died at the clinic, or something was happening with the family that I was struggling with. That instinct to reach out to my father was so strong — but I never got what I was looking for. He was never interested and the conversation would immediately turn to him and what he was doing and I'd be left listening on the end of the phone.

I've got friends who have awesome relationships with their fathers, and I'd see that as a young boy, watching from afar, thinking how cool it was. Their dads paid them attention, gave them time and affection, talked about good things with them, did things with them that didn't involve alcohol. I'd look longingly at those relationships; and even as an adult man it's still not easy to know that I won't ever have that kind of relationship with my father. But what is really lucky is that I've got my sons, and I do everything I can to have fantastic relationships with them. Even though I didn't have that for myself, I can create it for my children.

7 // THE GOOD MEDICINE

I was hardly a great catch. I was a 20-year-old with a declining career in the Customs Department, where I'd already had a warning for doing something stupid. And yet here I was about to become a father, and I felt so responsible.

I hadn't even shared with Tracy that I wanted to become a doctor. What could I have said?

Oh yeah, I applied to medical school but I wasn't good enough to get in . . .

But I wanted to be a great role model for my child. I wanted to provide everything for my new family. So I told Tracy that I didn't want to work in Customs all my life; I wanted to go back to university and become a doctor. It was a real leap of faith for her but she has always supported me.

Would I have ever gone back to medicine if I hadn't had kids at that time of my life? Who knows? That is the intriguing thing about life. Having kids gave me the motivation to transcend my lack of confidence.

The medical school said that to reapply I'd need to do a year of a science degree and then come back and see them. That seemed doable to me now, so to help my chances of success I enrolled in a summer science school at the University of Auckland. It was a full-time class, really basic, looking at the periodic table again, learning how to write an essay — which I was still crap at — learning how to study, and that gave me some confidence. From there I enrolled in a science degree, doing physics, chemistry and biology, as well as Māori language.

Tracy and Conor came with me to the interview. Numbers for some of the courses were limited and I had to convince the course directors that they should let me in. One of these directors looked at Tracy and Conor — there weren't many students who had a partner and baby with them — and I'm sure it was because of the two of them that he took a chance and let me in. I felt that was how it went.

During my first stint at Auckland University in 1991 I had had some mentors from the proactive Tuākana programme, which supports Māori through science degrees. This time, there wasn't anyone jumping out of the woodwork saying, *Man, you're so capable of doing this. Let's support you.* No, it was just Tracy and Conor, but that was good enough. The academic confidence might not have been there, but I had a good reason to keep going, to keep motivated, and I came home to it every night. Sitting in the lounge and studying in front of them made me feel so proud and excited.

Thanks to Tracy's savings and with some help from her parents we were able to buy our first house. She cashed in her travel ticket and we bought a dirt-cheap, run-down three-bedroom bungalow in Onehunga — just before property prices started to rise. To own our own home, to be able to improve it, to take pride in it — that was an amazing thing for us as a young couple. And because of that lucky start, we have only ever rented for six months in more than 20 years of marriage.

Tracy got a full-time job as a practice nurse in a clinic just up the road from our new house and, with help from both our mums, we managed. Conor had to go into daycare at about 10 months, so my mum Marlene would come all the way over to our house to pick him up at 7.30 in the morning, drive him to daycare in Howick, then Tracy's mum would pick him up at 4 p.m., and Marlene would bring him home to us at 6, when Tracy finished work.

Then we'd try to have some time together. Inevitably Conor would be up till 10 or 11 at night. But it was good and it was working.

I did well that year. I got As for chemistry. My poorest mark was for Māori, and that was because I was focused so hard on the sciences. It was time to reapply for medical school.

IT WAS JUST TRACY, CONOR AND ME. IT WAS JUST US AND OUR MISSION.

I was applying under the Māori and Pacific Admissions Scheme (MAPAS), which exists to increase the numbers of indigenous doctors. So I went down to the same marae I'd been at three years earlier. The first time I had had my good friend from school with me and we were super-confident young guys. This time it was just Tracy, Conor and me. It was just us and our mission.

First you have the welcome, where I did the mihi again, did the kōrero, and then you go into little rooms and get interviewed by a doctor, by a kaumātua, by a prominent person from the university, teasing out whether you're the right person to let in. The admissions process is designed to discover the wider things about an applicant which means not only that they'll be a great graduate but also that they're going to succeed. What's their family support like? What are the strengths they have to get through six torrid years of a medical education when times can get very tough? They no doubt saw the support of Tracy and Conor as being a potent source of motivation for me, and indeed that's really what got me through med school: Tracy and the kids.

I was accepted. I had six years of intense study ahead of me.

//

A medical degree is not an impossible degree, but it's a lot of work and it goes on for a long time.

Every year was drama. Every year was hard. Almost every year I said to Tracy, 'I don't want to go back next year. I'll sit the exams but I don't think I'll go back.' And sometimes I'd say, 'I'm not going to sit the exams because I think I'm going to fail.' It happened at the end of third year, fourth, fifth, sixth year. Tracy dragged me kicking and screaming through that degree. She said things that made sense: 'You've come too far. You're capable of doing it. Give it a chance. Just try, Lance, because even if you don't succeed at least you've tried.'

The toughest exams of all come at the end of the fifth year. Most people start studying on day one of that year, and halfway through they're doing mock exams. Not me, though. I was just trying to keep my head above water with the assignments and the mini-assessments, and the kids, with daycare drop-offs and pick-ups and nappies at night, and trying to be a husband to Tracy. So a month before the exams I hadn't even begun studying.

'I can't do it,' I told Tracy. 'I've done no study for the biggest exams of the course. Look, maybe it's best I pull out now and start again next year . . .'

She'd heard it all before.

'No,' she said. 'You're going to get in there and you're going to do it.'

She locked me in the study, brought me food, and left me to it. So I focused and ended up doing really well. The exam results came out and I was like, *Wow*. I got a B plus, and I was really happy with that.

But still the anguish and uncertainty continued.

I was so afraid of failure I would rather not even try. I'd rather not do the exam than say I'd failed. Of course, I know now that this is not a good strategy. The thing was, I had so much self-doubt. To get anywhere, you have to believe in yourself. But this is a challenge if you are someone who for whatever reason doesn't have self-belief. For me, the reason was that I always felt in catch-up mode. My education had effectively begun at 15, yet I was surrounded by people who had been to top schools and were high achievers and had bucketloads of intellectual confidence as a result. Some of the schools had streamed the kids to get ready for medicine when they were two years out, while I was still trying to get my head around how to actually get through the university system. I never felt I was as good as them.

Even in my final year, just six months from finishing my training, I went to one of the deans and said, 'I think I'm going to pull out of medical school this year, maybe think about coming back next year.'

He just said: 'OK, well, see the lady at the front with your paperwork.'

I was stunned.

Is that all? You're not even going to fight? You're not even going to stop me?

I couldn't figure it out. And I thought, *Well, I'm not going to give in just like that!*

It was Tracy who got me through, and this is what I say to young people now when I'm talking to them: the people around you can enhance or diminish your self-belief. It is so important to recognise that, and to be around others who will support you and encourage you, and enhance your self-belief.

Of course, I was also older than the other students — my fellow school-leavers were into their third or fourth year by the time I finally arrived at university — and I had a different background to most of them. Also, I was a family man, so I didn't do all the things everyone else did. It set me apart, but I felt really proud about that — proud that I knew who I was and was clear about the direction I was taking.

My friends from Hato Petera and even the guys I played league with were putting energy into football and partying but I had a family and full-on medical degree to get through. I remember thinking how cool it would be to go out and play with them, or chase the pot of gold in Australia, or play high-level league, but I decided to invest in medicine, to give it a go.

So, Tracy and I took it year by year.

//

Meanwhile, we did some property development on the side. In the holidays we painted the house inside and out, polished the floors, did the gardens, painted the roof, and then we sold it and made quite a lot of money because the market had started to climb. Next we bought two 100-year-old villas next door to each other, again in Onehunga, one of them tenanted by Highway 67 gang members. We moved into one and started doing up the other.

I hadn't enjoyed my first year of medical school so it was easy to convince myself that I needed to leave uni for a year and take on the job of doing up these villas. We had got into a bit of strife with money, and I persuaded Tracy it would save us from financial ruin if I could work on the houses instead of paying someone else to do it. I wasn't a builder but I could figure out how to run a string line, put up some posts, put up a fence, put some pavers down, plant some trees, strip and paint the house inside and out. I loved the physical work. As much as I love working as a doctor, I really love hard, physical labour.

By that stage Tracy was pregnant with Te Miringa. We were on a roll now and we'd decided to go for it, so this new baby was not a surprise. When Te Miringa was six weeks old Tracy went back to work on reduced hours and during weekends because the rate was better, and I brought Te Miringa in for feeds. By the time Tracy got home I'd have the kids bathed, fed and ready for bed. It was chaos but somehow we pulled it together.

At the end of that year I was pretty keen to get back to my study.

Tracy continued to work part-time and be at home with the kids. What with the higher weekend rates, the student allowance and an accommodation supplement, we were all right. We weren't well off but just spent a lot of time at parks and playgrounds, having fun for free.

We sold those villas and decided we were over old houses. We moved to Panmure, where we bought a four-bedroom cedar townhouse. We had our third child, Nina. Somewhere in our fourth year we seriously thought of moving to Dunedin, to the Otago Medical School, but we weren't able to get approval from the universities. We had our eye on a bluestone four-bedroomed villa on 10 acres for $150,000. If we'd moved south, our story could have turned out very differently.

//

Right up to the end, I doubted my ability to finish medical school. I doubted myself right up to the moment when I found that my overall grade for my final year was A minus. The whole time I'd looked up to other students who I thought were super smart, and I'd felt inferior to them — and yet some of them got lower grades than mine. *Really*? That was so hard to take on board. Could it be that I actually was capable after all?

FAILURE HAD BEEN A REAL OPTION FOR ME. THERE WERE SO MANY TIMES I COULD HAVE JUST WALKED AWAY FROM MEDICAL SCHOOL SIMPLY BECAUSE I DIDN'T BELIEVE IN MYSELF AND MY ABILITY TO DO WELL.

By this stage we had four kids — Conor, Te Miringa, Nina and Te Hira. There had been times when I couldn't get to lectures because I had to take care of my children, and I was far from the perfect student. Nevertheless, I'd got a result that I was more than happy with. And it was over and I was so proud.

At our graduation I was asked to do the opening mihi, and the Hippocratic oath in Māori. That was the beginning of a sense of health leadership — it was the first time I spoke as a Māori doctor.

Fifteen years earlier, the best that people seemed to hope for me was that I would stay out of trouble. Now I was a doctor.

I believe my story holds meaning for others — certainly for young Māori who, like me, witness the evidence of failure among our people, their apparent inability to succeed, and who take that model of failure into their own lives. I was now strong in my Māori identity — it was such an important part of who I was and what I was seeking. Yet I was no doubt affected by the general idea at large in our society that being Māori in New Zealand meant you couldn't be a success. Failure had been a real option for me. There were so many times I could have just walked away from medical school simply because I didn't believe in myself and my ability to do well.

And this is where my story also has meaning for non-Māori, for any young person who is struggling with self-belief. I hope they can see that someone who suffered greatly from lack of self-belief managed, with support, to keep going and eventually achieve success.

//

There is an incredibly small number of Māori doctors. We're 2.9 per cent of the medical practitioner population, yet Māori are 15 per cent of the overall population and 30 per cent of the sick population.

MAPAS, the scheme through which I gained entry into medical school, addresses head-on this lack of Māori and Pasifika doctors. It provides support for people who otherwise might struggle in the university environment, for all the reasons I've already mentioned — lack of opportunity for rigorous academic learning, lack of positive role modelling, an over-abundance of failure. Entry requirements are very slightly lower than for general admission, but once you're in you have to achieve at the same level as everyone else.

It's a good system because we need more Māori doctors. You could do away with MAPAS if you could prove that students coming out of medical school were all culturally competent and able to deal with our people and relate to them in a way that is helpful. You could do away with MAPAS if society was more equal — but it's not. A lot of the kids who make it to medical school have had access to really good standards of education, whereas a lot of Māori students haven't. They're behind from the start. So schemes like MAPAS are about trying to get them in the door.

So, I'm a Māori doctor who went through a preferential admission scheme designed to increase the number of Māori doctors. It's worked really well in my case because I'm a person who's come back to our people. I'm dedicated and committed to improving New Zealand society through my work in Māori communities. But, surprisingly, that outcome doesn't happen by design. It's by choice.

There's no obligation once you've been selected by the MAPAS scheme to give anything back to the community that enabled your entry to medical school. After all your training, there is nothing to stop you heading for the Gold Coast where you can earn maybe double what you may earn here. What a waste of an opportunity for our country.

But medicine is a public service as well as a career choice, and I think the terms of the preferential admission scheme should reflect that. When someone signs up for preferential admission into medical school, they should then sign up to contribute back. It would be entirely optional. The options would be: you can apply to medical school through the mainstream selection process, in which case you have no obligation; or you can apply through the preferential admissions scheme, in which case the quid pro quo is that after your training you are bonded to work in an area of priority for Māori health. If you are going to get into medical school under such a scheme, then your priority is not to go to London and work on Harley Street, or Australia where you can make half a million bucks a year. Your obligation is to give back to your community — the community whose needs the preferential scheme was created to serve.

I think we should strongly encourage people to stay and do a return of service. We help you. You give something back. The question is how do we make it attractive for them to stay?

I came up to the Far North — a stressful, high-needs area — when I was still a relatively new doctor. I wanted to work in this kind of community, and I was told there was a doctor with 20 years' experience who would support and mentor me. He left a week after I got here, leaving me to run clinics up and down the peninsula with no supervision, no mentoring, no encouragement. That experience leads me to think that you could attract younger doctors to stay and contribute in areas of high need by giving them a supportive environment that includes senior mentors. This system would recognise that these doctors are young, they have energy and passion and skills; that they are the future for this area. Instead of being thrown in the deep end they'd be working with someone who can support and influence them in a positive way.

I do believe that we need to match the MAPAS scheme with a return-of-service obligation. But in my case, I was passionate about making a difference among my people, and I couldn't wait to get started.

8 // ROTORUA: A LAUNCHING PAD

S tudying medicine was hard enough, but putting it into practice — oh my gosh.

I've got to look after this patient. Their health is in my hands.

It's such a responsibility.

After completing a medical degree, new graduates have to work in a hospital for two years to complete their training. We applied to five hospitals and I got four offers, including one from Rotorua Hospital. We accepted it, which was the best decision. We ended up spending four and a half years in Rotorua and it was a wonderful time and, of course, Tracy was happy to be among her family.

Rotorua felt like the right place to begin my career, because even though there's high need among large numbers of Māori in the community, it is a well-supported environment where I could cut my teeth, in medical terms.

And we wanted our kids to be brought up knowing about the places they're from, and to feel strongly connected to them. A lot of times you'll find kids are lost because they don't have a connection. That's a really big problem for our people. So many kids born out of wedlock, who don't know who their father is, don't know their whakapapa, and so they're just drifting. Neither Tracy nor I had grown up knowing about things like that, but now we were passionate about our connections. Rotorua was an important place to begin, but we both knew it wouldn't be where we ended up. I was beginning the process of researching my own whakapapa and I knew I wanted to practise medicine among my own people eventually. But at that time we grabbed the opportunity to be among Tracy's whānau, especially her grandmother, who was very elderly.

We rented out our house in Auckland and bought an old bungalow that stood on a 2 acre block about 15 minutes out of town heading towards Whakatāne, in a really pretty place called Tikitere. It was off the road and it was ugly, but it was a real steal. We built an amazing vege garden with raised beds, planted an orchard and hedges. We kept sheep. One year, from our four or five ewes, we had 14 lambs, and the kids would go out and feed them, because a mother can't feed four lambs at once. We had an old ram called Shags and he was like a machine, really good at his job.

//

Working in the hospital's emergency department, I realised that emergency medicine was the ambulance at the bottom of the cliff. Hospital medicine in general was reactive instead of proactive, and I slowly figured out that the best fit for me was general practice, where I could do the preventative stuff.

Thinking about my career path I considered what would help me as an individual, what would help my people, what would be best for my family. There are quite a few options for a young doctor to consider — surgery, public health, psychiatry, emergency medicine. One by one I crossed them off.

The trouble with surgery is that it ties you to the main centres, and I had dreams of bringing up my family in a rural environment.

If I became a public-health physician I'd be sitting in a university or a government department, or maybe in a district health board (DHB) office, and I'd be one step removed from actual patients — real people struggling with real problems.

I did a stint at inpatient psychiatry and it surprised me that I liked it. There's a whole lot of talking that needs to be done with the patient, teasing out what their mental-health problem is, and I liked the fact you could deal with a range of people from different walks of life. Māori rates of mental illness are really high, and I thought it would be cool to bring a Māori perspective to this. However, the focus would, of course, be narrow — just mental health.

A LOT OF TIMES YOU'LL FIND KIDS ARE LOST BECAUSE THEY DON'T HAVE A CONNECTION. THAT'S A REALLY BIG PROBLEM FOR OUR PEOPLE.

I was increasingly drawn to general practice. I liked the variety — that you could be seeing a surgical patient, then a mental-health patient, and then a paediatric patient. I'd be involved with women's health, with public-health campaigns. I would be seeing really sick people and really well people. In the hospital's emergency department I'd see the same person coming in with asthma five times in a month. I knew that as a GP, I'd have a chance to engage with that person and make a difference to their health before they got to the point where they found themselves in an emergency department.

I was keen on the idea that as a GP I would be working with whole families, not just one individual. And I knew that as a GP I'd be able to work anywhere in the country. It ticked a lot of boxes for my family, and for what we wanted to achieve.

I got accepted into the GP scheme and then began on-the-job training, working for six months each in two practices.

First was with a Pākehā doctor, Clem Le Lievre, of French heritage but who'd come up to Rotorua from Southland. Within a couple of weeks of starting work, Clem gently challenged me. I'd go into the waiting room, say the patient's name and then I'd introduce myself: 'Hi, my name's Lance, come on through, have a seat.'

Clem said to me, 'Oh Lance, I thought you'd say kia ora to your patients.'

I've got a Pākehā doctor from Southland telling me how I should interact with Māori patients!

Then I thought, *He's right!*

Next I worked with Dr Bernard Conlon at his practice in Murupara, a small town between Rotorua and the Urewera that was hit hard with the loss of forestry jobs in the late 1980s. Although there's a strong sense of community there, the town struggles, the population is poor and 80 per cent of patients are Māori.

I felt a real affinity with Bernard's Irish heritage. Our Irish heritage was really important to my mum and her family. When I was at primary school, people used to tease me with Irish jokes, which I found upsetting without really knowing why. *How do you sink an Irish submarine? Knock on the door.* I'm as proud of my Irish heritage as I am of my Māori heritage, but the Māori side gets more prominence because of the context I live in.

I KNEW THAT AS A GP I'D BE ABLE TO WORK ANYWHERE IN THE COUNTRY. IT TICKED A LOT OF BOXES FOR MY FAMILY, AND FOR WHAT WE WANTED TO ACHIEVE.

Bernard was amazing in terms of his commitment to his community. He taught me a lot about passion for the patients, and he knew all his patients personally. The way I deal with my patients now, making connections to place them within their extended family — *Who's your mum and dad? Oh so you're that one? I know your mum and dad, how are they?* and so on — that was him. He had a real warm way about him.

After the year of training I sat some pretty big, wide-ranging exams, and then I was able to apply for a proper job of my own. I was accepted by the Māori health provider Korowai Aroha, in Rotorua.

I still had heaps to learn about the needs of the communities that I hoped to serve. I had a romantic notion of what medicine was for: patients would come in, we'd patch them up, we'd send them home, they'd listen to what we said, and do as we suggested. This relied on the assumption that I understood what the problem was and on the patient's ability to address it.

Even coming from the background I did, it took a while for the penny to drop that this person was going to a home with a lot of social issues which were going to affect how much information he could absorb, how much medicine she or he could afford, or whether they could actually manage to access the care I'd recommended.

Even though I'd done my apprenticeship I was still pretty raw. I had a lot to learn about life in the trenches.

ROTORUA HAS A HIGH POPULATION OF MĀORI, BUT EVEN SO WHEN I WAS AT THE HOSPITAL I WAS ONE OF ONLY TWO MĀORI DOCTORS.

Also, I was now a doctor and that very fact set me apart from the people I most wanted to work with. Compared to them I was highly educated and very well paid, and they might well perceive the differences between us rather than the similarities. I try quite a lot in my practice to decrease and diminish this hierarchy of professional and lay person/patient, because that can be quite harmful. I try to say, *Hey, I'm a doctor, but also I'm like you.* That said, it's hard to balance the relationship.

For instance, when I started at my first job as a GP, I thought it would be a good idea to present myself casually. I went to work in jandals and board shorts, topped with a Hawaiian shirt. I had long hair and a goatee, and I thought, *Yes, I'm more like the people that are coming to see me.* I thought if I looked and sounded more like them I might reach them more easily, or they might feel more comfortable. It was a while before I realised that they expected to see a professional — a professional doctor coming across with competent, clear messages. I realised my casual dress was distracting. Instead of listening to me, they'd be thinking, *Man, he looks like he just got off the surf. He's very casual — is his advice casual, too?*

So I changed my way a bit there. To be respectful.

This was echoed recently at an indigenous medical practitioners' conference where a woman said the exact same thing: 'I started wearing a business suit to my job as a medical receptionist 27 years ago because that's what my people deserved.' Now she's the CEO of a huge indigenous health service in Alaska.

Rotorua has a high population of Māori, but even so when I was at the hospital I was one of only two Māori doctors (the other was Ranginui Walker's grandson). I was proud to be there, and determined to make a difference. Soon after I arrived I was interviewed by a journalist from the local newspaper and the resulting article was headlined: 'Making a difference for my people'. Somebody wrote me an anonymous letter, enclosing the article across which they'd scrawled: 'O'Sullivan?? Will you be going to Dublin to treat "your people?"'

They'd missed the point.

//

This was a time of becoming more politically aware. In 2004 there was enormous Māori protest over the government's attempt to claim ownership of the foreshore and seabed. Our whānau was invited to join the hīkoi that was travelling from the Far North down to Wellington. I went along as a doctor to look after the old people and anyone who was sick, but no one needed me. They were all too excited and busy.

We marched down Queen Street in Auckland with Tracy's grandmother, whom we called Nanny Mac — her real name was Riparata Macfarlane. She was then well into her nineties. It was very special. Then we hopped in the car and rejoined the hīkoi at Rotorua, then again in Wellington.

It was a significant point in the history of Māori nationhood. We had so many Māori come together. Some reports said 50,000 were in the march by the time we got to Wellington. Fifty thousand people in one place for a common reason, a common goal. And out of that the Māori Party was formed. It was a milestone in the history of Māori political conscience.

//

We all loved Rotorua, but it wasn't long before I had the opportunity to take a job in Kaitāia. It was what I wanted — a job in the area my own family had come from, near where my grandmother was born, in a district where Māori made up half the population and had high, unmet needs. Better still, it was with a Māori health provider, Te Hauora O Te Hiku O Te Ika.

Tracy was sad to leave our house. She had just given birth to Wairua right there at home. It had been such a happy time for her. She hadn't had to work outside the home, and had thrown herself into the kōhanga and the school, where the kids were in a total immersion class. She was absorbed in the life of her family, visiting her nanny who still lived in the same old house she'd always lived in, across the road from the airport.

So we never did get any of the fruit off the trees we planted there, because before they grew into maturity we had sold the house and moved away. Sometimes now we go back for a look, and the smoke is coming out the chimney, and the hedges have grown, and the trees are fruiting.

—

HE AHA TE MEA NUI O TE AO? HE TANGATA! HE TANGATA! HE TANGATA!

//

WHAT IS THE MOST IMPORTANT THING IN THE WORLD? IT IS PEOPLE! IT IS PEOPLE! IT IS PEOPLE!

—

PART 3 //

MĀORI DOCTOR

9 // IT'S ABOUT MORE THAN JUST LABELS

always wanted to come up to the North.

In our Auckland days we camped up here every year, right from when Conor was about two, and pretty much every year after that. We'd go every summer to Mataī Bay, or Tauranga Bay, Matauri Bay, Whangaruru North Head. We always loved it — who wouldn't? It's a beautiful area, and perfect for kids.

My grandmother's connection made it seem like home, and all the time while I'm out and about in this landscape, I imagine what it was like for my ancestors.

When I look at this land I bring the understanding I've gleaned from each of my heritages. I think of my grandfather on my mother's side, who came back from the war and cut a farm and a livelihood out of a gorse-covered block of land in South Canterbury with a bullock and handheld implements. There's lots of evidence of similar effort in the Far North. And then there's my connection to the land and tangata whenua, from a time when there weren't fences and boundary lines. There were sites for the collection of food, and sites for sacred events, and sites for living, and even today there is evidence of that living, the pā and the villages. I drive past mountains that are terraced and shaped. They are a clear reminder that this is where our tūpuna stayed — an imprint left on the land.

WE'VE MADE IT OUR PLACE AND THIS IS OUR HOME.

These things are constant reminders. Sometimes I look at the pā sites that have cows shitting all over them and I think it's a real shame. It's a shame they're not treated with a bit more reverence.

//

Living in Kaitāia was tough to begin with. I was a young, inexperienced doctor. I felt isolated, and a few months after we moved, when Tracy and I were walking on Ninety Mile Beach, I said, 'I don't know if I can stay here. Maybe we should go back to Rotorua . . .'

'No,' she said. 'You brought us up here. You've got to make it work because I'm not moving again. You're not going to give up that easy.'

That was really brave of Tracy, because I knew how much she'd loved living in Rotorua. If she'd said, 'OK, let's go,' that would have been it. But instead she was really firm: 'Just handle it and get on with it.'

I think deep down that's what I wanted to hear, and so we did stay, and, of course, now we've made it our place and this is our home.

It took a while to get settled. One of the reasons we moved was because land was so cheap, but by the time we arrived property prices were peaking because the avocado industry had taken off. Land prices were crazy but after a lot of looking we found our house. It's 15 kilometres out of town — a really ugly, orange-painted brick house surrounded by massive pines. But it was on 4 acres and it was really quiet and a few years later when we cut down the pines we got a beautiful view of Lake Ngatu.

I love living in rural New Zealand. I've got so many opportunities for fresh air, to get out on a bike and not get run over by the 1000 cars driving past, or asphyxiated by the smog. At the end of each day, when I head out of town towards home, all the stresses of my job seem a bit less. I know I'm going to a place which is a little bit insulated from the dramas of my work. Being a doctor brings a very heavy burden, and while it's not like I forget about all the suffering when I'm away from work, it's really important for my mental health to have a physical distance from everything that's happened in the day.

Tracy and I have travelled a little in the last few years. We were in Paris on the Champs-Elysées and around the Arc de Triomphe and it was awesome, of course — the crowds, the buzz of a historic city. But when we got home and drove into Kaitāia down the main street, and it was a Sunday afternoon and there was hardly anyone around — all you needed was tumbleweed to blow across the road and the picture would have been complete — I realised that I love this place. For me, it is the Champs-Elysées of the North.

Kaitāia is a long way from anywhere else. It's very different from Rotorua. In Rotorua, because of tourism, Māori culture is celebrated. On every billboard someone is doing a haka or having a hāngi, and there are images of beautiful, strong Māori everywhere. Certainly in Rotorua there are a lot of whānau who struggle but you also see a lot of well-off and educated Māori, proud of their culture.

In the Far North there are lots more whānau who are poor and hardly any that aren't. Everywhere you go you see people who have it hard. It took a while for the true extent of poverty in Kaitāia to become clear to me. I was aware it existed, of course, but for the first few years I must have had filters on. As I got more involved in children's health, especially the tragedy of rheumatic fever, I realised that behind much of this illness lies poverty. The issues that drive it are not medical, they're social — poor housing, low incomes, low levels of education and limited access to healthcare.

So I got to know my patients. I also started playing rugby for the local team, and our kids were playing sport too. Conor was ready to go to college and we sent him up to the kura, the school run by Hone and Hilda Harawira, and we started to meet people from there. We went to hui. We met lots of people through kōhanga. We went to tangi. We got more and more involved, and the community became our community.

No one knew anything about me when I arrived. Although my grandmother was born just south of Kaitāia, and her mother was born in Kaitāia, the contact with whānau had been lost in the intervening decades. So me coming back to Kaitāia was a real lost son returning, and I was very grateful for the warm way my whānau and I were welcomed.

There was no longer anyone alive who knew my grandmother. However, the family itself — Rapihana or, in the English transliteration, Robson — is well known, so I could connect with the wider iwi on that basis.

It's one of my great pleasures to talk to people as I meet them, either in my capacity as doctor or just as someone active in the community, and to discover connections. Someone remembers my grandmother's sisters. Someone else comes up to me and says, 'Hey, we're related through this family person or that family person.' In Māori culture it doesn't matter whether you're one or five generations apart; people readily make the connections. It's an honour and such a rich experience for me. It's about street credibility.

Re-establishing these connections is important and acts against the tides of recent history. Communities have shattered and dispersed, the network of relationships has been torn, but just as our family has in one generation reclaimed te reo and our tikanga, we are also reclaiming our relationship to this place, these people, this history.

//

When I graduated from medical school, I thought I would just fall into a system that would be pleased to have me and would allow me to effect the changes I thought I was capable of, with the skills that I had. While I knew the system didn't work for Māori in mainstream settings I was sure it would be different working in a Māori organisation. It was interesting to find that it wasn't — and that realisation didn't just come on the strength of one experience with one organisation, but over several organisations.

I realised that it takes more than just changing the colour of the people delivering the services to actually effect real change. It's not just a matter of putting Māori labels on buildings and doors and cars. It's actually about asking, 'What doesn't work for Māori in the mainstream health system?' There's no point just replicating something that doesn't work. We have to examine it closely and try a different approach.

This is what I observed. When a health system waits for people to come to it, many leave it too late. People who live in poverty are stressed. They don't know where the next dollar is coming from, and their lives can be quite disorganised because of this. Maybe they don't even have a phone, or they do but it's only got 50 cents credit on it and they can't afford to wait on the line for the receptionist. Or they know they owe the practice money from the last visit so they're going to get turned down for an appointment anyway. All of these things can make a doctor's appointment a bridge too far.

At Te Hauora O Te Hiku O Te Ika I had a daily appointment list of 25 patients. Of those, five — maybe even 10 — would not turn up for their appointment. There could be myriad reasons why they didn't. If they couldn't make their appointment they couldn't let us know because they didn't have a phone. Or they had no petrol in the car and couldn't afford to get into town at the appointed time.

These people have so many barriers to healthcare, and one of them is that medical practitioners have a rigid and inflexible system of booking appointments. Doctors schedule appointments to suit themselves, and patients are given options within that. It looks like a choice but it's not a real choice. If you ask a patient what's the best time to be seen . . . *Well*, they'll say, *I'm calling now*.

When a healthcare system becomes doctor-focused rather than patient-focused you get situations like one I saw when someone turned up to an appointment and took 10 minutes to limp up the ramp and into the surgery, whereupon they were told to rebook because they were 10 minutes late. Yet another patient not being allowed to access care.

Or a patient rings the doctor and is told it's two days before they can be seen. One guy with severe abdominal pain was told he couldn't be seen for three days. I couldn't believe it. I felt the culture was unfriendly towards patients — and that in itself could be enough to put people off coming.

//

Māori health providers have an interesting history. Mostly, they started off being run by nannies and aunties who came together, found some premises in which they could offer some services, and then worked on a voluntary basis. They were very much about using that inherent skill they had as Māori women, to talk to other Māori women about the importance of Pap smears, or immunisations, or diabetes education and so on. They weren't doctors and nurses but community health workers, going into homes and trying to get Māori to engage with health services. They were about addressing the disconnect between Māori and the healthcare system.

My Auntie Nellie, the one who took me to the hui where I met my 45-minute man, was part of this push to connect Māori with health services. She is a hospital-trained nurse — of all the 18 children in my father's family she was the only one to get any education or training after leaving school — and was one of the first women in the Waikato responsible for getting Māori women into cervical screening programmes.

Te Hauora O Te Hiku O Te Ika, where I now found myself, had exactly this history. But, as happened nationwide, things became more complicated once we dived into the sometimes poisoned chalice of funding. The need for compliance around contracting turned these simple organisations into complex ones — and I believe that's what set Māori health providers on the path to becoming like mainstream providers. Contracts are prescriptive and it doesn't make a lot of difference which organisation is bidding for them. They limit the opportunity for Māori or any other ethnic group to find their own solutions to the issues which their own communities face.

Certainly, at Te Hiku we offered mainstream services with just a few differences. We had a lot of Māori nurses and a lot of Māori community health workers and Māori managers. However, I was the only Māori doctor — the first in its 25 years or so of operation. I was a rarity. Which made it doubly offensive when I was told I was no less and no more important than a recently appointed American doctor. My experience with my patients was that they responded very strongly to having a Māori doctor who could speak to them in their own language and understand something about the context of their lives.

I became quite disparaging about Māori health providers. I didn't think they were capable of achieving the gains Māori people need. However, on reflection I've softened my stance on that a little bit and have come to the realisation they are still evolving. They've been in existence for only 20 or 30 years and it's a big challenge to create a strong infrastructure and workforce in that time, or to effect change in a group of people where there are significant disparities. I acknowledge the value of services that are set up, governed and run with a vision to improve in particular Māori health outcomes.

What I would say is there is a really important need for Māori health providers to have strong and confident political, financial and community-led governance, and then obviously the same for their health workforce. I think those things are still not quite there.

As the years passed — almost six years since moving from Rotorua to Kaitāia — I became increasingly despondent about what I was achieving as a doctor. I could see where the system wasn't meeting the needs of our community and I found it frustrating. I could see ways we could improve outcomes, but my employer wasn't interested in my ideas.

//

In the downtime when people didn't turn up for their appointments, I was getting paid well to sit on Trade Me and Google when I should have been doing my job. I was training for Ironman races, googling the latest carbon-fibre bike and planning where in the world I would race. But it wasn't rewarding — not rewarding for a person who came to medical school wanting to help people.

I used to say to the managers of that clinic, 'Look, why don't we change our model? Why don't we improve our system?'

But I just got pooh-poohed: 'Everyone's too busy, we don't want to change the way we do it.'

It was the same with other ideas. I'd say, 'Can I come and present an idea to the managers' meeting?'

No.

I was passionate. I had all this energy and these skills and I wanted better health for our people.

No.

I tell you what, I used to beat my head in frustration.

One time, I'd had a really exciting idea about how we could fight rheumatic fever in our community, setting up a scheme to test kids in school, catching the disease in its early stages so the children wouldn't go on to get life-debilitating illnesses.

No.

So rather than see this opportunity pass out of our area, I approached a local rūnanga and suggested they take on the contract.

Yes, they said.

The crunch came with the clinic when I insisted on treating patients even if they had unpaid debts. I felt that money shouldn't be an impediment to healthcare. The clinic strongly opposed that.

Tracy and I talked and talked. She said, 'Just resign. Leave. You'll find another job. Something will work out.' So I did.

But no one offered me a job. None of the other clinics were interested. Maybe they thought I was too much trouble. 'Maverick' was the word my old employer was using to describe me.

We seriously considered moving to Australia. I looked into getting my Australian medical registration. Tracy and I really pondered it. Should we just follow the easy route? We've got a family; if we go we can give them the best opportunities in life. We could just work hard and do well for ourselves.

But I didn't go to medical school to end up working in Australia, serving a well population and getting highly paid. Even just talking about it I felt like a Judas, turning my back on what I had dreamed of doing and being.

Meanwhile, the issue between me and the clinic hit the national news. The question — why would a Māori doctor who has such a passion for working for his community finish working for a Māori health provider? — was sparking a lot of interest. The *New Zealand Herald* and *New Zealand Doctor* covered what was happening, alongside articles about Māori health and the increasing poverty gap. Māori Television's current events show *Native Affairs* covered the issue several times, bringing their cameras up to Kaitāia and using the hook of my conflict with Te Hiku to also focus on the issues around poor health and housing in our community.

Haami Piripi, chairman of northern iwi Te Rarawa, told Radio New Zealand the issue lay with Te Hiku's policy of turning away patients who could not pay. He said that while I took the Hippocratic oath very seriously, the priority of Te Hiku management was to keep its accounts straight. Clearly, passions were running very high in the community.

The issue really put the spotlight on local access to healthcare. Radio New Zealand also talked to patients who wouldn't have been seen if I hadn't gone against the wishes of Te Hiku and treated them anyway. One patient told the station she had been turned away by the clinic because she had no money that day. I had seen her anyway and identified a serious health problem, but the receptionist warned her she wouldn't be seen again until she'd paid her bill. They also spoke to a father who had brought in a sick child for treatment. I had noticed the father was also unwell and treated him, although he could not pay. To me, I was just doing the job of a doctor.

I found I had a lot of support. It was very, very humbling. A local teacher, Vaniva Lewis, went public saying the fees were beyond the reach of many whānau. She organised a petition calling on the Te Hiku board to be more accountable and transparent. Some patients organised a march, and one of them, Mere Simons, told the *Northern Advocate*: 'If I can march to Wellington for the foreshore and seabed, I will surely march for Lance to tautoko, to show our support for him . . . He belongs here, he's Te Rarawa.' There was even a public protest held outside Te Hiku's offices, and someone set up a Facebook page to support me, which got 1700 'likes'.

Many patients rang our home during the day, wanting me to continue being their doctor.

'I can't,' I said. 'You have to see one of the other doctors at the practice.'

'No,' they replied. 'You are my doctor. I'm not going to see anyone else.'

Finally Tracy said, 'Why don't we just open our own practice? I mean, how hard can it be?'

10 // TE KŌHANGA WHAKAORA

What do we think our people need; how can we deliver it?

We decided to be courageous and embark on a pathway of making a difference. We realised we could set up our own clinic which would provide our answers to these questions.

We borrowed some money and created a company, Navilluso Medical Ltd, and rented some rooms at Kaitāia Hospital. It was perfect — being in the hospital meant we could be a real one-stop health shop for our people. Hector Busby, the renowned navigator and master waka builder, gave us the name for our clinic: Te Kōhanga Whakaora (The Nest of Wellness) and the logo was a gift from local artist Theresa Reihana.

There was quite a bit of continuing media interest in what we were doing. *Native Affairs* came up to Kaitāia again and did a story on our new clinic, and I told them: 'We'll talk about fees but if you're going to turn up here to see me today and you're sick but you have no money in your pocket, am I going to turn you away? No way!'

WE JUST OPEN OUR DOORS AND PEOPLE CAN COME IN WHEN THEY NEED TO.

The clinic was our bricks and mortar; we would bring to it all the tikanga and ambience that we felt our community deserved.

In my younger life I had wondered what it would be like to own my own business. Now here we were doing it, and many aspects were terrifying: the harsh realities of self-employment, of employing other people and being responsible for their livelihoods. People resigned from jobs to come and work for us — could we really give them job security?

There was no manual on how to open a high-access, high-quality health clinic in the Far North. We often asked ourselves, 'Where are the people who support initiatives likes this?' We had to organise our licence, sign authorities, negotiate contracts, write job descriptions. We were like any small New Zealand business trying to get started. But we were a business that believed we could affect social change. We employed people who were unemployed and unskilled. The qualification they had was that they could communicate with the people we needed to reach. We did not go through a medical course to open a business, but our experience showed us that this was the way to influence change.

On the opening day, many community leaders and people from Kaitāia turned up to welcome us. They walked through all the rooms, and Hector Busby did a blessing. I said my hope was we'd hear our language flying and floating around the hospital, comforting our sick in their beds, and also that the hospital would be seen as a place to maintain wellness rather than only a place to come to die. We had lots of support, and lots of people registering with us — and we've been busy ever since we opened our doors.

//

Once we were in charge of our own clinic, we could try anything we thought might improve our people's access to healthcare. It wasn't rocket science and it wasn't even all new. We were just trying to shift the model of care a bit. If we thought something was a good idea for our community, we would give it a go. That's the beauty of running your own business. So the first thing we did, from day one, was provide a walk-in system.

We don't have any set appointments in the mornings. We just open our doors and people can come in when they need to. When I come into my clinic in the morning, I don't know if it's going to be a quiet day or a busy day. Will there be no patients, or will there be 50? It's a little bit radical and a little outside our comfort zone. And typically our days are always busy, because we've created a system that's really easy for people to use exactly when they need it. I think that approach empowers our patients.

For the first four months I did a day's work in the clinic, and in the evening worked in the hospital to cover the bills. We paid our staff, which to begin with was about 10 full- and part-time staff, with borrowed money. But I believe that in 20 years' time, when we reflect on how hard it was in the beginning, we will have grown into a significant health organisation with a worldwide reputation for innovation, for pioneering smart ways of doing things. We will be proud.

The clinic has been a massive change for Tracy — in fact, for all our family. She went from being an at-home mother to working full time in our practice. She was our receptionist, then she took on the payroll and the accounts — while still trying to do everything for the family. It was pretty crazy. Lance, our youngest, was still at kōhanga, and the boys would catch the bus to school, then sometimes they'd all go to friends after school until Tracy could pick them up after work. We'd all get back home late and there would be no dinner ready, and, not surprisingly, Tracy was finding it hard to do everything.

A year after we established the clinic, we approached my mother Marlene, who at that time was still living and working in Auckland, and asked if she would come to live with us and hold the fort at home. So that's what's happened and it's a fantastic arrangement. Mum lives in a little caravan a few metres away from our back door, although she is planning to build a cottage on our property. She organises the kids to and from school, bakes cakes, cooks meals and, as a really smart health promoter herself, is a great contributor to all the ideas we need for our projects. We are very lucky.

Eventually Tracy realised we could pay someone else to do the money side of things, and she was freed up to become the project manager, dealing with staff and patient issues, and writing funding applications. She works in the territory not just of what we are doing, but what we are going to do next. She's become so much more involved in my working life, and that's really cool. Our business has never just been 'I' — it's been 'we' from the beginning.

We're a good team. I'm good with ideas, but Tracy knows how to get things done. For instance, I said to her one day, 'Wouldn't it be awesome if we could develop a strategy to eradicate the superbug MRSA from homes. We could pilot an initiative and if we could prove to the government that it worked, it could become a national initiative.' It was a pipe dream.

'OK,' Tracy said. 'Cool.' She canvassed some medical students and found one she thought was amazing and was keen to do the work. She liaised with the Health Research

Council, an academic supervisor and the funders who could actually make it happen — even to the point of making sure the student had accommodation up in Kaitāia. And now we're getting research done and have hopes of developing a programme that could make a big difference.

Tracy makes things happen.

Having the clinic has reignited my passion. I recognise that I've been through a cycle: I went to Hato Petera and I was inspired; my passion was burning brightly. I went to medical school and I learned a lot about Western medicine and Western models of care: the passion got compromised a bit. I worked in the system and my passion was compromised further. Then it required a step up, quite a bit of courage and risk-taking, to say: *This is not what I want to be remembered for*. Now we offer models of care that are a little different to general practice, but totally responsive to the conditions we see around us. Once again my passion is burning brightly.

//

Einstein said it best. He reckoned that the definition of insanity is doing the same thing over and over and expecting a different outcome. This is absolutely applicable to healthcare. The health system works best for the people who probably need it the least, but it doesn't work for the people who need it the most. Māori health is far inferior to that of non-Māori. Do we really think that if we keep doing what we've always done, suddenly one day Māori will be equally as healthy as non-Māori ? Something we're doing isn't working — so we have to think of different ways of doing it.

We have a great health system in New Zealand that employs highly skilled people. It serves many people well, but out on the margins is a sizeable group that it doesn't serve well. We're keen to serve at those margins.

When we opened Te Kōhanga Whakaora we didn't want to replicate what everybody else was doing. That said, we are a general practice clinic and probably 70–80 per cent of what we do is the same as everybody else. But the balance is our crucial difference — that's where we find innovative ways of helping our high-needs patients. We're always looking for new ways of meeting those needs.

Bureaucratic thinking is the enemy. It's beaten into people until they become slaves to the idea that we have to do things as they've always been done. The system is rigid and inflexible, and patients have to conform. We say that's rubbish. We want to be able, within our means, to conform to the patients' needs. We are looking at ways we can do that.

For a start, 90 per cent of our staff are Māori. As 95 per cent of our patients are Māori, we feel we have an appropriate workforce for our population. If you look at the national average, a practice might have 15–20 per cent Māori patients. I would be really surprised if there were many practices or health services around the country that had 20 per cent Māori staff. We have a good balance. The same should apply if I was a doctor working in a community that was 95 per cent Chinese.

If you think of the usual GP practice, it will have a receptionist, a nurse and a doctor. However, for a practice such as ours, I don't believe that model provides the kind of healthcare experience that our people need. What's essential for our patients is having people who may not be highly clinical but who can help make their health journey a lot more comfortable and a lot more rewarding. Therefore, we have a real focus on employing a workforce that our community can relate to.

So we employ people we call kaiārahi, which means navigator — someone who plots a path. Kaiārahi are laypeople — home-grown in our own community — whom we train in healthcare assistant-type roles to deliver simple healthcare such as checking blood pressure and weight. But they actually have a more important attribute, very different from a diploma or a degree: they relate well to our patients. They can talk to our patients about heart disease and heart health, for instance, in language that our patients feel comfortable with.

Two years into our organisation's existence we employ seven kaiārahi. We do a lot of staff training, and some go on to further study and qualifications. A couple of our kaiārahi weren't working at all before they came to us. Now they work 8–5 Monday to Friday. One of them is a very capable young woman who will go on to train as a nurse practitioner, and we'll support her through that. Another kaiārahi is a nursing student.

The health sector in general would do well to review the mix of staff they have, and consider that relying on clinicians doesn't answer all the needs of a community.

This isn't to say that technical skill and expertise aren't important. Of course, they're critical. But a more crucial element of our service is that a patient communicates with someone they know, who talks like them, thinks like them and whom they can understand. Once we've got that right, we know we can do a better job of transferring expert skill and knowledge.

We are always making changes to our structure. It's one of the really great things about having our own business: if we want to make a change to improve our outcomes, we can just do it. We have to figure out the right formula for the people we serve. If something doesn't work we change it. We learn from our mistakes, but when something is successful we say, *Hey look, we did that as a team.*

We are always looking at new roles for our business. For instance, we have employed two nurse practitioners — advanced nurses who can do many things a doctor can — to run our walk-in clinic and help manage our chronic-care patients. This takes a lot of pressure off me, and frees me up to be more strategic about patient care.

The walk-in clinic is a big part of our practice, and is often the point of initial contact, where we first hear about a patient's particular problem. But we can't deal with people's health just helter-skelter on the day. After their walk-in appointment, we've got to get them back. We've got to educate our patients about the importance of self-management. If I was minister of health, I would be asking, *What is the single most effective way of reducing health costs in the future*? Well, number one is prevention. Number two is getting patients to do more for themselves. If I could give a patient who's got health problems a kit of equipment that would allow them to manage their health at home, to take more control over their health — whether it's blood pressure, weight or blood tests to measure their diabetes — they could do those things without a doctor being involved. That would increase the patient's control over their health. This would lead to better health outcomes and would cut the cost of our health system. The future of our health system has to be built on more patient involvement in their care and less reliance on traditional models of thinking where doctors and nurses are seen as the oracle of healthcare.

We want to offer people the opportunity to be seen when they need to be seen. After the morning walk-in consultation, we need to find a time for people to have a sit-down appointment, in a measured way. The access to acute care is important but we also want to retain the traditional model of general practice where you have a booked appointment that is not rushed: you see your doctor, you talk about your health plan for the year. We say, *What time does it suit you to come in and see us*?

It's so important to engage with people on a number of levels. Diabetes care demonstrates this really well. For instance, if I or another educated person had diabetes, which is a chronic disease requiring constant care and overseeing, we would take our medications, we would plan for when our medications ran out, we would have an understanding about what all the measurements meant for our health: the two levels in the blood pressure, protein in the urine, the blood test, why eye-screening is important, why foot checks are important. We'd know everything about all those things.

YOU LEARN SO MUCH MORE FROM GOING INTO A PATIENT'S HOME THAN IN THE ARTIFICIAL ENVIRONMENT OF THE CLINIC.

But what typically happens in our community is our patients know nothing about their condition or how to manage it. They run out of their meds on Tuesday morning and when they get up the next day there is nothing to take. Traditionally, they would ring up the doctor for an appointment, but they might not be able to get one for a few days, and in some cases it can take three or four weeks. So they'd go without their meds for that long.

In our clinic they can walk in any morning and be seen. We say, 'OK, you've run out of medication. We're going to give you your meds today because it's important. But we're also going to book you in for an appointment that suits you, because we need to sit down with you and talk about the importance of not leaving things till the eleventh hour. If you treat your condition like that it's going to be a poor outcome for you as an individual, a poor outcome for your family and a poor outcome for our system because in five years' time you'll be on dialysis, which costs $50,000 a year. That's not a good outcome for anyone, because the life expectancy of patients, once they start dialysis, is five to seven years — a massive loss to us all.'

We have to provide a mix of care. Because we're passionate about improving outcomes, we've got to try some new things, sharpen some of the old ways and stick with the others. We've got to keep trying until we've got a system that works well. When we treat someone, whether it's for a skin infection or diabetes or whatever, it's part of a health journey. It's never just a moment in time.

I want to do more house visits. You learn so much more from going into a patient's home than in the artificial environment of the clinic. We've got around 3000 patients in around 600 homes. It's not feasible or sustainable to think that every appointment could be in a patient's home, but over time I would like to visit each home, especially those with young children. It wouldn't be too hard to create a schedule for that. People are grateful that you make the effort to come to see them.

I want to offer free healthcare to anyone in a Women's Refuge, and free and accessible healthcare to children in Child, Youth and Family (CYF) care. If you are in a refuge or under CYF care you should have a dedicated, passionate health service to meet your needs because you are vulnerable. You are the most vulnerable person in our country. And what happens at the moment? In an after-hours emergency, CYF don't have anyone to ring. People ring whichever of the 12 local doctors is on call. They ring a doctor who might not really want to see them but because they're on call they have to. I think that's bad.

I want our mums and kids who are in a Women's Refuge to know that we're here because we care about them. We'll come to a refuge or a neutral place or, if they ring up, we arrange whatever healthcare they need on their terms, because we believe they are in a real crisis. People only end up in a Women's Refuge if they are in crisis.

I can imagine a time when we employ someone to manage the day-to-day running of the clinic. But not yet. We're still in a phase of exploration and testing things. But when we feel we have nailed 80 per cent of what needs to be done, I would really like to be able to hand over the reins to someone and tell them that this is the trajectory we are heading on, just keep us there.

//

Our profession is a caring industry, by definition. We talk about healthcare and medical care and primary care and secondary care, yet I think the caring aspect of it gets lost in translation. Really caring for people, seeing and reaching out to the individuals who are sitting in front of us, forming a connection with them — goes against the paradigm of clinical practice. Some people say that what I do at Te Kōhanga Whakaora is not what a doctor should be doing. Effectively, they say I care too much, and get involved in parts of my patients' lives that doctors shouldn't take a professional interest in — their family situation, the kind of houses they live in.

I chose my career, my profession, to suit the person I am, to allow me to use the passion I have to effect the outcomes I want to achieve, and to make use of the inherent qualities I bring to this world. Maybe some of the work I do is outside the narrowly defined role of a doctor, but for me doctoring has always been about far more than just the individual in front of me — it's about all the environmental factors that have caused this person to experience illness. Being a doctor gives me leverage, it gives me status and credibility and the means to achieve what I want to achieve.

Māori culture is an intimate culture. We touch a lot. When we greet people we'll hongi or kiss, we shake hands, we put our hands on people's shoulders, we embrace — and this extends even to people we're not very familiar with. I really love that about my role, being able to demonstrate warmth to people in my clinic and in my community. Kuia and kaumātua can see me as one of their mokopuna, and I'll see them as one of my elders, even if we have no blood links. Equally, I talk to rangatahi. I ask who their parents are, and find a connection. I'll often say to them, you're the same age as my son, or my daughter. It's the personal aspect of what our profession is about.

I show my patients that I am a caring doctor. With a teenager who has been sexually abused and who suffers from depression, I shake his hand, look him in the eye and say, 'I've noticed you around town, and I'm glad you've come to see me so that I can help you. You're a good young man, capable of great things, and I'm going to help you and I'm committed to doing that.'

Of course I give him really clear professional assistance, too. After talking to him and seeing the results of the depression questionnaire he's filled in I know it's important that he begins taking medication. I explain it won't start working immediately, but that he needs to see me on a regular basis for a while, and I set him up with a nurse in community mental health who will monitor him while he takes the medication, and who he can build a relationship with.

I say, 'I'm really keen to help you achieve your potential, and we'll do this by catching up regularly.' There's no point being a nice, warm, fuzzy person and then just saying casually, 'Let's see how things go'. It is important to have a good plan that this patient fully understands.

Some people say that's really personal and crosses the boundaries of what a doctor is supposed to be and do. But the way I see it is that my qualification puts me in front of this guy, but then I can also use all my inherent qualities and passion to help him. I *want* to help him.

Another young guy came in to see me. He had a brain tumour and it's left him with some problems, but I consider it my job to steer him away from a state of mind that accepts he's going to sit on welfare for the rest of his life. I tell him he's a fine, strong young man with a smart head on his shoulders and he needs to get out into the world. 'You're nineteen and I don't want to see you in a rut of welfare for the rest of your life.' Then I say, 'There's no charge for today because that's my way of helping you.'

I offer clinically sound care but I wrap that in genuine care. *You do matter. You do matter to me.* I'm not going to call you at home every night and I'm not going to get really deeply involved in your life, but I am a doctor who cares for you.

//

I don't subscribe to this idea that we treat everyone the same: 'I'm not going to treat Māori different from Pākehā or Pasifika or Asian people; I treat everyone the same.' That's not tenable for higher-needs communities. We need to be as sharp as possible when it comes to understanding the type of community we serve.

We sometimes have staff — Pākehā and Māori — who say, 'Look, Lance, we've got someone who owes a lot of money, we don't think they should be able to get an appointment until they've paid it off.'

I say, 'No. That attitude is a hangover from your experience in a health service that hasn't served our people well.'

When I was working in the rigid health system, if you owed money, you would be questioned, interrogated and humiliated at the front desk. I saw the resulting sense of shame drive people away from much-needed healthcare. That sense of shame would stop people bringing their child to the doctor. I saw that. It makes access to healthcare for higher-needs and vulnerable communities potentially humiliating, a threatening environment.

Luckily, in our practice we've got the ability and autonomy to decide how we want to do things, and how our staff will behave towards our patients. I have a lot of trust in my community. If I see a patient who owes me money, I think, *That's all right, they will pay the account in time.* I might give them a gentle reminder though: 'We actually do need you to help pay your way. It's also important for you to invest in your health. If you put a little bit into your healthcare, I believe you will get that back.'

I'm really happy that I can say to my patients who don't have any money on the day, 'Just pay when you can. I know you will fix it up.' And they do.

It's not a big deal and I try to get as much funding from elsewhere as I can, so that patients who can't pay don't have to. I strive to provide a culturally competent health service that meets the needs of the community.

The girls in the office laugh and say, 'You know how much we banked the other day? Eighty dollars.' Yeah, but we get money from the government, and we take a lot by EFTPOS, of course. We're not starving, we pay our staff. I'm not stupid, and, actually, I do have a business focus — I want to run a successful practice that can go on doing good. There's no point in us having to close in a year's time because we've been too Robin Hood in our approach.

We get money from those who can afford it. If the government gives us money for doing particular things well, then let's do those things really well. The other thing is, I work really hard — probably as hard as two doctors. That saves a salary. I work hard all day and then I get home and work some more.

//

I am often required to complete medical assessments for people who are on sickness or invalid's benefits. It is a task I dread. There is a lot of pressure to make decisions that I feel uncomfortable about. The Work and Income NZ (WINZ) officers tell my patients to take the form to me and get me to sign it. I find myself in a situation where I'm putting my professional standing at risk by signing something I don't think is right. This form says they're incapacitated and I don't always think they are.

It is actually rare that someone is truly unable to work due to severe medical problems. Most of the assessments we are asked to do are more influenced by the terrible lack of job opportunities, combined with a sense of dependency that has been created in communities, sometimes over generations.

I challenge my patients: 'Part of the solution is that you have to wake up. You have to stop this *I'm a victim, I'm entitled to things.*'

I say this all the time, and I lose patients because of it.

'I need a sickness benefit.'

'Why?'

'Because I have a chronic health problem.'

'OK. I see you walking around. You're smoking. You don't work and you get paid by the government to live at home. You have a health problem that I want to refer you to a specialist for and give you medication for, but you don't want to take it. You're making a decision not to take medication because of your belief that you don't want to poison your body, despite the fact that you poison your body with four thousand chemicals every puff.

'I'm one of your own. I'm going to challenge you. You need to get out of your rut. You need to get out of your dependency on welfare. You're a twenty-year-old guy who's had a catastrophic accident but you're now as good as you're going to get, and you've got to stop going to ACC and saying I need more, I need more, so you don't have to work for another five years. This is about you. You can make a decision to stop this.'

Another problem I often encounter is that some patients have already been wrongly assessed as unable to work by other doctors, and I become the bad guy who is trying to get them back to work. I think some doctors sign the paper just to get the person out of their rooms. That's the easy option.

I had a locum doctor working for me. A patient came in and said, in essence, 'I'm sick. I can't work.' The locum wrote one and a half lines and put her off work for two years. He disempowered my patient. He didn't even address her chronic lung disease.

But I said to her, 'You *can* work, even if it's ten or twenty hours a week, because the research shows that if you're involved in work, whether it's voluntary or paid, your symptoms, your mental and physical health are actually better, because you have a reason to get up in the morning. The routine of work gives you far superior outcomes from a health point of view. If I tick a box that says you can't work for two to five years, I'm taking those possibilities away from you.' The awesome thing was that the patient agreed. She was happy to do something. If you actually give people a choice, many make good ones. I think we rip people off too often by not having that conversation in the first place.

This is not an issue that should revolve around whether or not work is actually available. My job is not to say there's no work available. My job is to say if there is work, you're eligible, you're fit, and from a medical point of view you will be better out in the world than sitting at home.

This is an area where iwi could step up. They could get a workforce together, giving each person 10 hours a week work. It doesn't have to be paid, it could be voluntary, working in our community, painting our marae, cleaning our marae, putting in a garden, whatever. Let's use this workforce, which is already there in the Far North, to build our cultural strength again. To be honest, if that means they make no more money than what they get sitting around at home then it's still a win. In every way our people will be better off, and that will have flow-on effects into their families.

I was a product of the welfare system. My mother was on the DPB and I know that welfare is an important support for those who are vulnerable and in need, but it shouldn't be a career. It shouldn't be an entitlement, an expectation, no questions asked. There should be responsibilities. People are sometimes surprised to hear me talking like this. But I'm about empowerment, and that is the basis of my attitude to welfare benefits. Sometimes people need the empowerment that a benefit can bring; sometimes people need the empowerment of getting back into the workforce, and regaining their tino rangatiratanga.

Besides chronic pain conditions, people often seek a benefit because of drug and alcohol addictions. I am very happy to provide these people with short-term sickness benefits to support their recovery as long as they provide me with evidence that they are seeking help from, for instance, the Salvation Army Bridge Programme, Alcoholics Anonymous or DHB alcohol and addiction services. That is how benefits should be used — to help someone in a time of need.

And sometimes great things happen. I had a young patient who had been on the benefit since he was in his late teens. He came to get his medical certificate signed so he could get his benefit renewed for another three months. When I raised the point that his medical problems were not severe enough to make him unfit for work, he was relieved. He told me he really wanted to work and went away excited that a doctor had encouraged him to do just that.

As a caring society we are obliged to support those with severe medical problems in the best way possible. However, we need to ensure we are not giving people a shovel that digs a hole they can't get out of. We need to give them the opportunity to get back in and be a part of normal society.

//

Our receptionists sometimes tell me they have a problem making appointments for our patients because they only want to see me, who they know, and not the other doctors who work with us in the clinic. The responsibility weighs on me. I am like a shepherd and I want to look after my flock. If I give them to someone else they will manage their healthcare differently. Yet we have to make this practice bigger. We have to get more doctors. It is our challenge — that patients will come not because it's me, but because the experience of being in the clinic is enough to bring them in.

A really important focus for us is to make sure our staff are on board with our ideas, and that we in turn listen to our staff so that we are all moving in the same direction. Every Tuesday morning we have a staff meeting before the clinic opens. It's a chance for us all to discuss how things are working or need to be tweaked. Anyone can share new ideas.

We employ about 20 people now, half in the clinic and half off-site working in the community. I'm trying to inspire them all to think a little bit creatively about how we do things, and to inject passion into people.

Some people have passion as an inherent quality of their

personality. With others, I'm trying to flick the switch — which can be hard when people have been beaten down in a system. If you've been in the health system, you might think, what's the point in going that extra yard, because we're fighting a losing battle? I try to get my staff to see beyond the person sitting in front of them, to deconstruct their own thinking as health workers, to look beyond the way they've been trained to deal with issues.

We talk about broad ideas. For instance, we took our clinical nurse leader to a conference in Melbourne, and she reported back to the rest of the staff about how excited she was to listen to ideas about creativity and innovation. She gave a talk at our meeting about the value of breaking out of established patterns and looking at things in a fresh way. 'People think of creativity as a random occurrence but there are structured ways of being creative,' she told our meeting. Ideas like that spark important discussions among our staff.

Together we discuss why we do things. Income is one reason and that's fine and necessary — but we want to create a deeper and more profound 'why'. We try to find joy and meaning in our work, even though the work is often stressful and heartbreaking. We remind each other of our successes. I like the idea of beginning each meeting with a story — something that has happened in the course of our work, perhaps an interaction with a child in the clinic or through one of our programmes. It's so relevant because it reminds us of the humanity of healthcare. This is different from the technical skills required. Humanity is the difference between a good health professional and a great health professional.

For the last part of the meeting, just before the clinic opens, we get outside and walk. A walking meeting. We breathe fresh air and we exercise. We are good role models for the rest of the community, and there's a different quality to our conversation as we walk.

//

It is the nature of our job as doctors that we deal with life and death. I've made some choices that have been life-saving and I've made some that were not. We do our best, but sometimes the situation conspires against us. We always feel unhappy and disappointed in ourselves when we don't get the results we are after. That emotion is stronger than the emotion of celebrating when we have done well. I've saved lives but I tell you the ones that are at the front of my mind are the lives that didn't turn out the way I'd hoped. Here's one example.

I was asleep in the hospital staffroom one night when, around two o'clock in the morning, a nurse burst in saying there was a child who was not breathing. I was still half asleep as I ran out to the resuscitation room in the emergency department. Sure enough, there was a little girl with this horrible pre-terminal breathing. The child had been brought in by a family member who told us a story about how the injuries occurred. It turned out that the child actually had been severely abused.

We did everything we could but we couldn't save that child and the other staff present and I had the horrible experience of trying to save a life in vain, when there is nothing you can do. The child died while undergoing a CT scan in Auckland a few hours after leaving us.

I was traumatised by that experience — one of only two times in my life where I have been traumatised. The first was when my mother was assaulted in that random attack by a man who came into our house when I was small. That time I had flashbacks, was unable to sleep and suffered terrible fear. It was the same with this murdered child.

In those awful moments, as we tried to resuscitate the child, there were a whole lot of challenges going on for me. There was the clinical challenge: can I save this baby? Initially, I was the only doctor there and I was just trying to do my best to keep her alive. Then there was the shock: oh my gosh, what happened here? This is not an 80- or 90-year-old who has lived their life; this is a young being. I struggled with the knowledge that I had a son the same age. When I saw my son's face it was hard not to see this child's face. I found myself crying on my bike ride to work, having flashbacks of the events that occurred that day. And then it was traumatic all over again because we had to relive it with the police, giving a blow-by-blow account of what we did and what we saw and how things unfolded. And then we had to go to court, me and a couple of nurses, and that was traumatic again because we had to read our statements and relive it once more.

I suspect that as health professionals we don't do enough to take care of our own psychological health. I am considering getting myself some time with a clinical psychologist — someone to download with and work on some good strategies for putting things in perspective, so I don't end up a cot case at the end of my career.

//

I work at least 70 hours a week, often more. I've been blessed (or tortured) with incredible energy, but there's a breaking point and I think I've been close to it, if not exceeded it, sometimes. The worst was when I damaged my shoulder playing rugby league with our teenage son. I needed a shoulder replacement operation, and by the time it was scheduled, the only other doctor in my practice had resigned and I was on my own. I had to go ahead with the operation, but I came back to work just two days later, with a pump to inject anaesthetic into my neck. I carried it around in a wee handbag while I saw patients.

As well as my clinic work, I was on call at the hospital. Six days after my operation we had one of the busiest days the hospital had ever seen. It got too much. I was wounded not only physically but in terms of my capacity and functional ability. I had these thoughts going around in my head — I just didn't know how I was going to cope. I knew I was in danger of collapsing.

Usually when I'm stressed I find that physical exercise is a fantastic outlet, but in this situation I couldn't exercise because of the surgery, and that compounded the stress. Then I'd come home and offload it all on the family. I got upset with everyone. They copped a lot. If that had continued, it would have been the classic burnout — all flash and flame and gone. I was so stressed I had no idea what to do about it.

Finally one day Tracy, Conor and I took a drive down the beach to Ahipara, the tiny settlement at the south end of Ninety Mile Beach. We can just see Ahipara from the beach near our house, hazy amid cloud and seaspray. We sat on the sand and talked and I told them how badly I was struggling. I had hit a wall. They saw that I needed help. Tracy made an emergency call to an agency in Wellington and we got a locum for two or three months. Straight away that took the pressure off. I saw a counsellor for a while and that helped me realise some truths about the way I was dealing with stress. I couldn't do it all myself. I learned a lot.

I learned the value of asking for support when you need it.

I've got lots of energy, and it's a real driving force, but it's quite an all-consuming thing that can eat me up, too. If the energy hasn't got something to be directed towards, it turns into a deficit. I can't sit still. So I can either burn it out physically or put it towards a really good project.

I do need to relax, but for me, that's about doing things with my family. When work is busy, it's family time that gets compromised. So in the weekend I say, 'OK, Trace, let's get all the kids in the car, get a Thermos and some sausages and the barbecue and go up the beach for three or four hours and have a fantastic afternoon.'

And that's, *wow*, that's credits in the happy bank.

Relaxation for me is also being able to come home and not talk about work. In the days before Tracy became so involved in our business this could be quite a hard thing. I just wanted to come home and not talk, because I had a turnover of patients every 15 minutes or every five minutes, all day. They needed my full attention, for me to focus solely on the one to three or even 10 issues that they had. I had to give feedback and respond in a way that showed I was engaged with them.

I would come home and Tracy would say, 'How was your day?'

'It was good.'

'What did you do?'

'Uhhh . . .'

I wouldn't want to talk about it. It was hard for Tracy, who might have been at home all day and wanted to have some interaction with someone other than children and, through me, was trying to reach outside of the house.

Now, the situation is quite different. Since setting up the clinic we've had so many exciting things going on with our work, our business, that there wasn't a space where we didn't talk about it. If we've got problems with staff, or a really exciting contract, the temptation is to keep talking it over, even at the dinner table, even when we're getting ready for bed. It is still early days for us, learning how to run our own business, learning how to balance work and family.

Finally, we recognised that it was all too much. We decided we needed some time when we got home to talk about non-work-related things. We need to wind down, get some rest. Now we hardly ever talk about those sorts of things at home.

11 // KAITĀIA DOCTOR: YOU CAN DO SOMETHING ON MONDAY

When you're a doctor in a small town, your office is anywhere from the main street, to the swimming pool, to the supermarket.

I was in the breakfast cereal aisle one day, seeking out a nutritious product among the many sugar-laden varieties, when one of my patients came up to me. 'Doctor, doctor,' he said, urgently. 'I've got a lump on my dick.'

I looked anxiously around to see if anyone else was listening, although he didn't seem at all worried. So there was nothing for it but to do an on-the-spot consultation. He described the lump and I referred him to a urologist, who I explained was a 'dick doctor'. It was a long time before I ventured back to the cereal aisle again.

Another time I was at the swimming pool when someone was rescued from the bottom of the pool. This person wasn't breathing, and I along with an off-duty murse and a senior and junior lifeguard did CPR for 20 minutes before the ambulance arrived. The only piece of equipment in the pool's medical kit was a one-way-valve face mask, but someone had put it on the wrong way so it was now unusable. So we just did chest compressions, which is the most effective strategy anyway. At least it was a chance to show the pool attendants how to do CPR correctly.

The person lived, and two weeks later dropped off some snapper to say thank you.

At the side of the rugby field, at the farmers' market — part of my work happens out of my office.

I'm thrilled to have a set of skills that allows me to help people anywhere, whenever my help is needed.

//

In Northland, 48 per cent of children aged between zero and four are Māori. This means that one out of every two children who turn up to my practice on a Monday morning will be Māori.

But by the time they get to over 65 years of age, the numbers of Māori seeing me on Monday will be one in eight. Between the ages of under four to over 65, the percentage of Māori in our Northland population goes from one in two, to one in eight.

There are a couple of possibilities for this difference. One is that a whole heap of people are leaving the region and never coming back. But the numbers of Māori aged over 65 are about 15 per cent higher in Northland than they are nationally, where it's about 9 per cent. So they're not leaving the region and going elsewhere in the country. They *could* be leaving the region and going overseas.

The other possibility is that premature death is contributing to this significant drop in numbers. Internationally, death under the age of 65 is defined as premature. Māori children are dying prematurely of accidents, asthma, child abuse, sudden infant death syndrome (SIDS), violence, pneumonia, meningitis, all these things. Then as teenagers and young adults they're dying of suicide and car accidents and alcohol-related injuries. As they get into their thirties, forties, fifties, they die from heart disease, heart attacks, from cancers and diabetes.

When we lose elders that young we lose their cultural knowledge and the integrity of whānau. At the individual level, those people miss out on years of life. And financially, after a lifetime of paying taxes, they die before they are eligible for superannuation and the right to enjoy their retirement.

It's my suspicion that the drop-off in population is directly related to our failure to grab health gains in the early years of childhood. This isn't the only reason, but it contributes to it. And when I talk to groups of doctors, I say: 'Three out of four Māori children who visit your practice on Monday will be dead before they are 65. My question to you is: how are you going to address that? How are you going to make a difference? You have an opportunity to influence that outcome, either positively or negatively.'

MĀORI CHILDREN ARE DYING PREMATURELY OF ACCIDENTS, ASTHMA, CHILD ABUSE, SUDDEN INFANT DEATH SYNDROME, VIOLENCE.

I'd like to add that whenever I talk about issues, whatever the figures are for Māori disparities, add a 50 per cent premium for the Pasifika population. Our Polynesian population has worse outcomes than Māori for rheumatic fever, chronic lung disease in children, heart disease, diabetes and diabetes-related complications, and so on.

It's part of my leadership to challenge my colleagues about these things, and also to give them some strategies. I know it's hard for any of us to see the role we can play in the big picture. If I just said, 'Māori disparities exist in the health system and you have to go out and tackle them' — well, who would know where to start?

But I can say this: You can do something on Monday, when Māori children come in your door. You can set an example. Be aware of the broader issues, and deal with them by properly managing a sore throat in a Māori child, or properly managing skin infections in a Māori child. You can manage your interaction with a Māori guy who's got gout and who therefore may be at risk of heart disease. Why not take the opportunity to check for heart disease so that his story doesn't become that he was seen five times for gout and then had a heart attack at 40 and everyone said, *I didn't know, it wasn't picked up.*

We always need to keep in mind the broader aspects of the health risks each person brings into the doctor's room.

//

Around the time I won a Blake Leaders Award in 2013, I had the opportunity to visit many schools, where I planted the seeds of dreams in children's minds. It's really powerful to plant those seeds because without dreams we can do nothing. For months afterwards, I'd have kids coming up to me to tell me about the dreams they had for themselves. *I want to be . . . I want to do . . .* Planting dreams is part of the fight against poverty.

There are three kinds of poverty we need to consider: material poverty, poverty of spirit, and poverty of opportunity.

Child poverty is a huge issue. Estimates are that we've got at least 250,000 kids living in poverty. In 15 years those kids will be 250,000 parents bringing 500,000 children into the cycle of poverty. There will be some exceptional-plus people who will step out of that quagmire, but most will not be able to.

This is what drives me. As a doctor I can patch people up, but I can't ignore the factors that lie behind so many of the illnesses I see. Poverty exacerbates illness, and infections become rampant in overcrowded living situations. It's easy to feel overwhelmed, but I try to combat that by looking for solutions. When I leave Kaitāia to talk to organisations and the government about what I see as important ways forward for our people, our children, I liken it to coming out of the trenches into a more strategic position.

The cycle of illness and poor health can begin even before birth. How many mums are getting pregnant who are not healthy to start with? If farmers want to get a horse or a cow or a sheep to produce the most healthy foals or calves or lambs, they give them the best pasture, make sure they're in the best physical condition, immunise them, make sure they're not stressed — and the farmers get incredible returns on that care.

Yet we'll get a woman who weighs 120 kilograms, who smokes and drinks and eats McDonald's three times a week. How healthy is her baby likely to be? Then we wonder why we've got kids who've got terrible skin conditions, terrible chest problems. We have regulations about how you should treat animals if you're a stud farmer, whereas anyone living in the most appalling conditions can have a baby.

One of the reasons we see significant health problems is that they start in the mother pre-conception and carry on antenatally and into the formative years of life. We're not paying attention to important environmental factors and the critical perinatal period of our newest citizens, and we don't insist on access to nutritious food. As a society we don't monitor what's freely available — and actually I wouldn't even say 'freely available'. The very worst kinds of food are forced down people's throats, with every corner dairy selling Coke and a pie for $2.50, and tuckshops in schools that sell rubbish. You can't separate these factors from the health problems that are rife in poor communities. If you took all these kids and you put them on an island where they ate good food, and had plenty of exercise and access to a warm and healthy sleeping environment, they'd be fine. It may sound like a ridiculous suggestion, but the idea is that we can give children this island paradise by way of bolder political will that carries legislation over the line. We can create healthier environments where it is easier for people to make healthy choices.

So, it's complex. Child poverty is not only a huge issue, but it's multi-layered. It will take years to resolve, and needs agreement across the political parties — an agreed agenda that is supported by whoever is in government, and where opposition parties can openly make a contribution to deal with child poverty.

I do believe we have opportunities to address some aspects of child poverty really quickly. I think an important step is to make schools the focus for more than just learning, by making them a hub for other social and health initiatives. We have some reactive approaches at the moment, like social workers in schools. Of course having access to social workers is good but they are only there to pick up on the ones who are facing crises.

Imagine if we went in there with preventative health measures — if we fed all of our poor kids. Full on, not just Weet-Bix, but three square meals. Health checks and all the children's health needs, including social issues, could be addressed while they were at school.

At the end of the day and at the end of the term they're going home to their families — which may be an environment that is impoverished in just one or maybe even all of the ways I mentioned above — but for seven hours a day, five days a week, 39 weeks of the year, we're taking them out of poverty.

Money-wise, certainly there's investment required, but it's far easier than trying to provide the families of those 250,000 children with jobs and better incomes, or trying to rebuild all their homes and find 100,000 new homes within five years. It's about trying to break that cycle of poverty, not just material poverty but poverty of spirit. Some of these kids simply don't know anything better and unless we show them the possibilities, they don't even have a chance.

We need policy and funding on this. But the schools themselves are already achieving amazing things. The decile 1, 2 and 3 schools educate the poorest members of our society. And it's here that the magic can happen. It's where it needs to happen. The commitment from principals and teachers in those schools is often wonderful. They are already the masters of doing things differently.

We want these children to dream. Just because you come from a poor background shouldn't mean that you can't have dreams for yourself. If you have no dreams, you have nothing to carry you into your own life.

However, I'm realistic about this. Every day I battle with the challenges of trying to do something extraordinary with people who are ordinary. You have to be extraordinary to pull yourself out of the quagmire of poverty. And that's not what believers in a fair and just society like me and so many others feel is right.

//

There's a young man who brings his little baby in to see me for its regular check-ups. He's so gentle with his baby, and he makes me reflect on all the good things about being a young father with a newborn child — the love, the protection, the hopes and dreams.

Of course, I see many parents who are doing a great job despite significant challenges and barriers. I see young parents doing a really good job despite being so disadvantaged. I suspect part of it will be that they come from good families — there are cycles of positivity and good parenting, just as there are cycles of negativity and poor parenting. Despite the fact that things are pretty hard and they don't have a lot of money, these people have core values, and genuine love.

But all too often I see the other extreme of the spectrum — the damaged, damaging men who don't seem to care that their children are running around cold and unsupervised.

The group that's probably the most concerning is the apathetic group of men in the middle — the ones who just don't have the motivation, that little bit of spark to get them over the line from being a zombie father, who's not really present for the children's and the family's needs, to one who could be great.

It's frustrating.

Wasted potential.

It's the emptiness when you look into a person's eyes, that's driven by poverty of spirit, poverty of wealth and opportunity, and personal history. *I can't do much about the world I'm in and I've just got to suck it up.*

I think those people could take charge of some aspects of their life. I want to shake them awake and say, 'Look, things are tough but let's just work at it, work harder, be a bit more disciplined.'

How much change can we hope to make in these families? Some parents seem hopeless and dysfunctional — so how much effort can we realistically put into that generation? But why should their children be condemned?

We have families in our society that we could pour infinite effort and resources into. We might aspire for them to become the perfect nuclear family, but I just don't know if it's possible. Instead, if we can't create the perfect nuclear family, we should focus on getting the best possible outcomes for children.

We have after-school care for the children of working parents; maybe that needs to be applied to those who aren't working, as well. Maybe it's better to have those children for as long as possible in environments that are positive. And the same for holiday programmes — make them available to more than just the kids of working parents. We should be doing anything we can to get these kids into a more constructive environment more of the time.

So if I was to throw something out there, it might be to get more vulnerable kids into more hours of preschool, which is sensible because otherwise those vulnerable children are sitting at home in the midst of dysfunction.

As well as this kind of direct intervention, there are some things we can do around empowering and challenging parents to do better when raising their children. There are some sensible policies out there that make sure people are using their benefit money for the right things: making it compulsory that if you're on a benefit you have to enrol your child at an early childhood centre, and with a GP, and that you have to consider important health and social matters such as attending school and getting immunised.

There is a young boy who stays with us at times, and we are very close to him. He's a very dear young boy, but he has been exposed to a number of concerning factors — drug use, lack of work ethic, violence, lack of interest in education or getting a job. Our goal as a country should be to reduce his exposure to substance abuse and violence, and help him develop a reasonable ethic to education and work.

This young boy lived with us for one year. We didn't want

to let him go, but we really hope his time with us has given him a sense of what the possibilities are. Our input has given him positivity, a sense of right and wrong. He's seen us go off to work each day; he's been part of our whole family routine — been sent to school each day to learn. He's spent holidays with us. He's seen me give Tracy a cuddle, and he's seen us treat each other with respect and have healthy relationships.

This boy is an example of who Finance Minister Bill English was talking about when he met with us in Kaitāia in June 2014. He said, 'Lance, Tracy, there are about 2000 kids in New Zealand that will cost the country $750 million over their lifetime in justice costs alone. What is more staggering is that we know just who they are.' We know it — so doesn't it make sense to spend more money on prevention and intervention, to help people before their illnesses become debilitating?

I'm not saying that everyone from these very dysfunctional families can or should be uplifted and spend time with families like ours. But I do think our effort and energy as a society should go into the children — and I think the answer probably has a lot to do with educational institutions, from preschool education on, with extended-hours care.

12 // MĀORI LIVE IN TWO WORLDS

A high percentage of my patients are Māori, so being Māori myself is an essential part of what I offer. Being able to conduct entire consultations in te reo, bringing a Māori worldview and having a knowledge of the issues that affect Māori, such as that a Māori kid with asthma will be five or six times more likely to die from it than a non-Māori, all makes a difference.

Having Māori doctors for a Māori population is really important. Research shows that regardless of how good we are, and how pure our intentions, we tend to shut down when we're dealing with people who are less like us. We spend less time, order fewer investigations, treat less and have less rapport — and this is both self-reported by clinicians and reported by patients.

With patients who are like us, doctors take more accurate histories, and therefore treatment is more accurate. If we don't have this rapport, we are less likely to ask people to come back. We might skip tests or say, 'Let's see how it goes,' rather than saying, 'I'd like you to come back.'

I have medical students who train with me, and I tell them that it's about being a Māori doctor, instead of necessarily being a doctor who is Māori. I say, 'You're a good doctor if your patients walk out that door feeling like they've had their needs addressed.' There's a lot we can do to train doctors to have better cultural competency in their interactions with Māori.

Making patients more comfortable is an essential part of improving access to healthcare. I can see how blown away the students are when they observe a consultation done entirely in te reo. They might not understand it, but they understand the patient's body language, and how the kōrero sets up a completely different environment.

WE KNOW FROM OUR CONTACT WITH OTHER INDIGENOUS PEOPLES THAT WHAT WORKS WELL FOR MĀORI IN NEW ZEALAND WILL WORK WELL FOR PASIFIKA AND OTHER CULTURES.

We take elements of marae practice into our clinical experience so that we can find out more about the patients before we start getting into why they are here. This is how I see it: a consultation is like a mini-pōwhiri. With a pōwhiri we begin with the karanga — we call the people to come in. Then we have a mihi — we greet and acknowledge the people we have called into our consulting room. It's a formal welcome where we might talk about who we are and who they are — whakawhanaungatanga we call it, and it's about establishing relationships. Then we have hongi, consecrating the sacred part of the karanga and whaikōrero. This may mean pressing noses — connecting. All these things can be incorporated into a medical practice. If we use that approach we become closer to the patient and have more therapeutic rapport, more connectedness, better outcomes.

It boils down to being really conscious of the person in front of you, and who they are. If you have a conversation with a Māori person they'll ask you who you are and where you're from. I see a light go on when they hear that you might share the same maunga, waka or ancestor. Often with non-Māori people the first thing they want to find out is what I do and how important I am, and when they find out I'm a doctor they have a certain response to me as a person — I wonder if their response would be different if drove trucks?

Some of the things we're doing to improve cultural comp-etency for Māori will improve our interactions with other patients, too. We know from our contact with other indigenous peoples that what works well for Māori in New Zealand will work well for Pasifika and other cultures and probably better for a lot of Pākehā, too. What we do is very different to the terrible attitude you sometimes come across in hospitals where people are referred to as their disease — the kidney failure in Room 3, the 43-year-old diabetic. Doctors can be robotic, mechanical in their thinking; they break things down into disease. Trainee doctors are at risk of talking about patients like they're not people.

Admittedly, medical schools have changed a lot over the last 20 years or so, when it was just the smartest kids who got in even if they had the wrong type of personality. Now they do a 360 on the kids, so the selection process is a lot better. But what I suspect is that we might have changed the selection process but we haven't changed the training. When I was at medical school, communication was an important thing, but it needs to be more important — really, we should be spending about a third of a doctor's education on how to communicate well with patients.

In our clinic it would be ideal for the GPs to be Māori, but it's not a necessity and, in fact, just because someone is Māori doesn't mean the fit will be perfect. What's important is how clinically and culturally competent a doctor is. If we don't have that nailed then we will continue to have gaps in communication and gaps in care.

//

Even I have had to deconstruct some of my assumptions about what I think I know. I'm a doctor. As a profession, we've got this expert knowledge, we're at the top of the food chain. It took me a while to realise I needed to think about what knowledge my *patient* brings to this hui, and what mana, and what pūkenga or expertise.

Some of my ideas are rigid — I question the ability of an ointment to treat cancer, for instance. Yet I have had to change some of my thinking. I've learned that I have to give more time and credence to what's important to my patients. 'Look,' I sometimes have to say, 'you're going to have to forgive me. I'm trained in a Western model of care. I don't know anything about rongoa.'

In Māori communities probably around a quarter to a third of people use rongoa, traditional Māori medicine, or alternative medicines, and are suspicious of drugs and medications and synthetic preparations that they see as poisoning their body.

It can be frustrating. I'll get the patient who doesn't want to take any 'toxic medications', yet smokes and drinks. This population's health literacy doesn't stretch easily to the point where they can comprehend that on the one hand random, controlled trials with thousands of clinical patients show that smoking kills one in two people; and, on the other, clinical trials show that the risks of aspirin medication are very, very low but the benefits are very, very high. They still see the aspirin as a poison.

Sometimes their resistance to seeing the doctor is because of context. They might be thinking, *I don't want to see the doctor because I'm just going to get told yet again that I'm fat and overweight and I smoke and I'm lazy and I should be more active and should eat the right food and I should just listen more.*

'If you just listen and do as you're told . . .' — people don't want to hear that all the time.

People are fearful of what you know and what you might tell them. Māori are not alone in this, of course. You would think that if someone was coughing up blood, or passing blood in their stools, or losing a significant amount of weight, they would be concerned enough to get assessed and treated early on. Yet time and time again, they don't. Patients say that they knew it was something nasty and they didn't want to come in and get it checked out. There is both denial and fatalism: *I've seen all my family die of cancer so I know it's what I'm destined for*.

I've had young men my age say, 'Our philosophy in the Far North, Lance, is we are here for a good time not a long time.' They've seen so many family members die young, they think anything over 50 is a bonus.

Most New Zealanders don't realise the extent to which Māori live in two worlds. It's both enriching and strengthening, and challenging, because those two worlds have such different out-looks. Māori communities are wary of the mainstream. I don't think it's at the front of people's minds but if, for instance, you listen to parents who don't want to immunise their children, there is obvious fear and suspicion in what they're saying. We were young parents who listened to and read the misinformation put out by anti-immunisation lobbyists, convincing us that we were putting poison into our children, and building on the sometimes natural suspicion that Māori have of the establishment. It was not until later in our parenting journey that we developed a more critical view of this information and realised that not immunising would lead to a widening of the health gap for our children and our people. We now immunise all our children.

We are trying to change those mindsets by changing the experience people have in the health system. I try my hardest. I wouldn't say I always get it right, but I always do my best to ensure a patient walks out of the room more knowledgeable, more empowered than when they walked in, and that their experience of the hospital is different from what they've had in the past.

13 // ORDINARY AND EXTRAORDINARY: SEARCHING FOR EQUALITY

When I talk to young people who are in a similar situation to what mine was — disadvantaged both materially and spiritually — I often reflect on my story and what I've achieved. Let's look at two types of families.

You come from a sole parent family, not much money, broken relationships. Much of your family is uneducated and you, too, have a rough path through education. Because of all this, you feel instinctively that the world carries very low expectations of you, and that in turn influences your own feelings about yourself. Then look at what you've achieved: you're a doctor, a lawyer, a teacher, an executive.

On the other hand, you might come from a family of two parents, middle to high income, education throughout the family. You go to good schools, get a good education, and are encouraged and supported to grab the opportunities that come your way. Look at what you've achieved: you're a doctor, a lawyer, a teacher, an executive.

The child from that first family is actually quite exceptional. They had to be exceptional to get from where they began up to where they are today. To be honest, you would expect someone who's had a smooth pathway to achieve their potential, because everything was in place. But you might expect the child from that first family to not succeed.

PREMATURE DEATH OCCURS TWO TO FOUR TIMES AS OFTEN AMONG MĀORI AS IT DOES AMONG PĀKEHĀ.

So I say, *I was exceptional.* I was exceptional to achieve what I have, given my beginning and all those barriers. But I don't believe that anyone, especially those from a poor background, should have to be exceptional to achieve in our country. That's not right. That's not fair, because not everybody has that extra 50 per cent or 100 per cent of oomph to get them across the line. And it's the starting line I'm talking about here, not the finish line.

What I'm trying to pitch is that we shouldn't set up a society where some people's starting points are so much further back than others'. I have flipped my thinking on this. I used to think that everyone should have the opportunity to end up in the same place. Now I believe that's not realistic or even desirable. We're all different, with different potential. Not everyone can be high-flying executives or academic scientists or leaders.

But everyone should *start* in the same place, because then how far you go depends on your inherent qualities and the other things around you that mean you will succeed or not.

At the moment, the kids who succeed despite all their challenges are truly exceptional because they have had to run further and faster than anybody else.

How do we achieve this great goal of an equal starting line? This is a potent question. I've heard people say it's discrimination to give some groups in society a helping hand that others don't have. I have even heard the word 'apartheid' used, and that's strong and emotional kōrero that doesn't stand up to even the most cursory examination. South Africa's apartheid system was based on a minority people suppressing and oppressing a majority people. That's quite different to having a majority group supporting a minority to do well; in fact it's the polar opposite.

What I hope to see in my lifetime is New Zealand's majority group valuing their contribution to the progress of our ethnic minority. It's not about anyone being more important than anyone else — it's about equality. It's about creating a level playing-field, and that requires a little bit of extra effort to bring people up to the same level.

I've heard it said that we need to move from talking about 'race-based' to 'needs-based'. Well, they are one and the same, aren't they? Take rheumatic fever — in New Zealand, 95 per cent of children who get this disease are Māori or Pasifika. So why not call the rheumatic fever campaign a Māori and Pasifika programme? We're calling an animal that has black and white stripes, four hooves and a mane, an animal with black and white stripes, four hooves and a mane — instead of calling it a zebra. We are not being honest about what the real problem is.

Say we had a health programme aimed at reducing pre-mature death among New Zealanders — that is, death before the age of 65 — and we wanted to target the people most likely to die prematurely. We won't define who they are because that would be getting ethnic-specific, and too close to race-based funding. But the reality is that premature death occurs two to four times as often among Māori as it does among Pākehā.

Fear is a potent obstacle to change.

Fear of losing. Fear of someone getting more than they deserve. Fear that I'm not as important as someone else. Fear of actually naming the problem.

//

We've got a really good healthcare system in New Zealand but it's not accessible to everyone. The big question is: how do we improve that access? We've tried a number of ways, some of which I've discussed in chapter 10. Some have been incredibly successful, and some we need to keep thinking about and developing. Basically, though, improving access to good healthcare is about getting off our butts, getting out of our clinic and into the places where people live, work and play.

In the case of kids, it seems a no-brainer to reach them through the schools. School is a great place to deliver health services for children — they're captive, they're there. It adds value to the school and the community, because the school becomes a place to keep children well — which in turn helps to support the good work of the teachers, because if we can keep children well they have a better chance to learn. Maybe that naughty kid down the back of the class is not so much naughty as distracted by illness, itching or hunger.

Poor health is a barrier to learning, and if we can identify and address the issues that create these barriers, then children are going to learn better — and isn't that what schools are all about?

//

New Zealand has unusually high rates of rheumatic fever compared with other developed countries. It is a Third World disease, and the worst affected areas are sub-Saharan Africa, south-central Asia, the Pacific — and the indigenous populations of Australia and New Zealand. In the last few decades the disease has almost disappeared among Pākehā, but the rates for Māori and Pasifika children are among the highest in the world — and have kept on rising throughout the last 10 years. Rheumatic fever is a disease associated with poverty and overcrowding; unsurprisingly, rates are 23 times higher in the most overcrowded fifth of New Zealand homes than in the least crowded fifth.

Rheumatic fever — a disease that permanently damages the heart through inflammation and scarring of the heart valves — usually strikes children aged between five and 14. Those children who develop heart disease will walk around with the equivalent of a 70- or 80-year-old heart for the rest of their lives. They have no energy, and their ability to live full lives is seriously compromised. It can be dangerous for women to have children, and even playing sport can be dangerous. People with the disease sometimes have cardiac surgery up to three times throughout their life. This is awful for the individual and their families, and a terrible burden on our health system.

It's pretty easy to prevent rheumatic fever: a simple test involves swabbing the throat for A streptococcus (strep A), which is the bug that, if untreated, can lead to rheumatic fever. In 2011 the Māori Party, and Tariana Turia in particular, were instrumental in getting funding for a rheumatic fever prevention programme for children in high-risk areas, and for antibiotics for those with strep A.

Nationwide, more than 10,000 kids were swabbed in 2012, and of those, more than 1000 tested positive for strep A in that year alone — that's a lot of children who may have gone on to develop rheumatic fever but who instead were treated in time with antibiotics. It may be a Band-Aid policy — the real work needs to be done upstream to address the causes of child poverty and social inequality, which contribute to these infections — but it's making a real difference in the lives of these children and their families.

//

One of our great successes has been our schools-based MOKO Programme, through which our staff visit each of Kaitāia's 14 primary schools three times a week. Since launching in September 2012, the Kaitāia MOKO team has detected 738 cases of strep A. The estimated risk of developing acute rheumatic fever with untreated strep throat is 1 to 3 per cent. That would mean that this programme has stopped between seven and 20 children in Kaitāia getting acute rheumatic fever. If you reflect on the eight children we diagnosed with rheumatic heart disease on our ECHO screening project in 2010, this represents approximately 800 children in Kaitāia who had untreated strep throat infections. Remember Michael Paraha? If we had been able to detect the presence of strep A and treat it with antibiotics when he was younger, he would not have developed rheumatic fever. He would not have had open-heart surgery at the age of 13.

We knew from our own observations and talking to teachers that hakihaki, or skin infections, and kutu, head lice, are also a massive problem for kids in our area. It seemed crazy that we were in there looking at throats when we could see kids covered in school sores, their heads scabby from scratching at head lice.

I was at Kaitāia Primary School one day talking to the principal, Brendon Morrissey. I noticed a kid whose head lice were so bad you could see his scalp moving.

'How come things aren't treated before getting to this stage?' we asked each other.

And I added, 'I want to do something about this.'

'Whatever you come up with I'd like to be part of it,' he replied.

So we negotiated to extend our services to checking for hakihaki and kutu as well. Now when our team takes throat swabs they examine kids for skin sores and head lice. Thanks to the charity KidsCan, they hand out basic medication kits comprising plasters, sanitiser, tissues, nit combs and head lice treatments.

The team takes photos of skin infections and texts them to me, and I either prescribe medications by return text or get the child to come in to the clinic if necessary.

We now visit all the primary schools in Kaitāia — which adds up to around 2000 kids — three times a week. Brendon believes the MOKO programme adds to the appeal of his school in the community, because parents know their children will receive regular and free health checks there. In turn, it has reduced absenteeism because kids are getting picked up before they get really ill — and that means they are getting a better education. Brendon's own two sons, aged 10 and eight, have been picked up for strep A and prescribed antibiotics. 'Frankly, without the MOKO scheme, my boys could well have gone on to develop rheumatic fever,' he says.

When people say we shouldn't run these programmes because it's the parents' responsibility to take care of their children, I feel very upset. How on earth is any of this the child's fault? The issue is not bad parenting; it's about what we can do for these kids.

//

I had a young Māori mother bring her six-month-old daughter in to see me. The baby had severe facial eczema and over the past three or four months she had seen several doctors several times. Nothing had helped. In the meantime, of course, this mother was being looked down on in the street, with people asking, 'What sort of mother would allow her child to have this on her face?' They were probably judging that Māori mother, thinking she was neglecting her child by not taking her to the doctor.

Three or four days after the mother brought her daughter to me and I had prescribed a new kind of treatment, the child's face was clear of eczema. The mother had been almost in tears when she first brought the child in to our clinic; now, just days later, she was in tears again — happy tears.

What made the difference? It wasn't rocket science. It's just that previously this child's diagnosis had not taken into account cultural factors, whereas I looked at her with my cultural lens on and said: 'This child probably has an infection called MRSA.'

Methicillin-resistant *Staphylococcus aureus*, or MRSA, is common among Māori and high-needs populations. We call it a 'super bug' and it's resistant to the usual antibiotic treatment. More than 20 years ago, around the time I first applied to medical school, this super bug had celebratory status. If there was one case of MRSA in a New Zealand hospital, wards would be shut down and special teams like something out of the blockbuster movie *Contagion* would go in and do a full clear-and-eradication sweep. Newspapers ran front-page stories about the dreaded MRSA infecting the hospital.

Of course, hospital management got it in the ear for allowing this to happen. Yet no criticism at all was directed at the real culprits — research institutes, agricultural and farming industries, and inappropriate prescribing by doctors over the decades since the arrival of penicillin (the precursor of modern-day antibiotics). To be fair, these alleged human perpetrators cannot be held entirely to blame for the natural evolution of one of the smartest organisms on the planet. However, giving cows, chickens and other farmed animals antibiotics just so the farmer can make more money from a fatter and more lucrative beast is nonsense.

From a doctor's perspective I know that how we use (or misuse) antibiotics can result in the development of antibiotic resistance and the likelihood of treatment failure. These days MRSA no longer causes widespread panic and alarm; it's now so common that we hardly bat an eye when we see it. This is a big problem. We mustn't take this bug lightly. MRSA can cause significant harm and I have seen it cause a tragic death here in Kaitāia.

The most common problem we see with MRSA is young Māori children with lots of hakihaki that are not getting better, despite seeing a doctor and getting antibiotics. The normal story is these kids (and sometimes adults) are left with irritating and often sore and weeping skin infections all year round. I see it so much I think I can smell an MRSA infection now.

When I met this little six-month-old, I was certain her problem was MRSA. So we took a swab, and sure enough got the confirmation. Then we were able to give her the right kind of medication and therefore the right outcome.

Do I think that child suffered because of a dismissive attitude by the person who was judging that child because of their social background? Yes, I do. I don't believe doctors and nurses always put the right lens on. They're just looking at the physical symptoms of disease, and not looking at the person in front of them, who has all these other things that they bring into the consultation room. This is called 'cultural competency' and the challenge is to get all health professionals to better respond to it.

There's a heavy burden that falls on people of limited means — limited income, limited education, limited understanding, limited resilience and limited reserves of everything. If we got MRSA in our house, we'd manage it: we've got two educated parents, a steady ship and not a lot of stress or drama. We have the means to do the things we need to do. But it probably won't even happen to us.

Problems like MRSA most often happen to people who are already struggling. Inadequate income, someone sitting on the couch not getting out there, someone smoking too much dope, kids truanting, someone getting a bit of a hit from someone. Then on top of it they get this infectious disease that will probably be around for six or 12 months unless you can Janola-bath everyone in the household, wipe down all the surfaces with an antiseptic solution every day for a week, put antibiotic ointment in the nostrils of every person in the household three times a day for a week, scan all the family for skin infections and take them to the doctor if they see them. All those things are hard.

We've got 150 patients with MRSA in our practice, half of them under eight years of age. But we know it's very hard for these families to eradicate this infection. That is why we are so excited about our new project to eradicate the bug from people's homes. As well as extending the way information is recorded across the different medical practices in Kaitāia, our idea revolves around someone actually going into people's homes and showing them what they need to do, as well as providing families with a complete pack of equipment for dealing with the bug.

I believe we'll show in 12 to 24 months that this is a cost-effective programme, highly appropriate for our patients. I think it's going to be a winner. This is us not just being same-old, same-old, but creating exciting opportunities to do good in our community.

So, cultural competency is not about *I shouldn't touch them on the head*, or *I shouldn't sit on the table* or *I should know to address a kaumātua and kuia like this, and a child like this*. To be honest, that's the frilly stuff. The tapu of our culture is very deep, and I don't expect people to know about all that. But I do want them, if they're a doctor working in this community, whether they trained in New Zealand or in the United States, to be very competent at understanding the conditions our people face. To do that, they need to be culturally aware and, again, it's not about being able to pronounce people's names properly — although that's a good thing to do — it's about clinical, cultural competency as medical practitioners.

Back in 2010, after we scanned the hearts of Kaitāia kids as part of the Heart Foundation screening programme and found eight who had undiagnosed rheumatic fever, I took the opportunity to do an audit on some of those children. Of those found to have heart damage, how many had seen a doctor complaining of a sore throat? Sure enough, some of them had come in two years earlier with a sore throat and seen their doctor, who had given them paracetamol and sent them home. So our health system was culpable. We contributed to that child getting rheumatic fever. The treatment was clinically competent, because in many situations that would be a perfectly fine way of responding to a sore throat, but the diagnosis was cloaked in cultural incompetency — a doctor looking after high-risk Māori children in an area where rheumatic fever is rife, but looking with the wrong lens on.

Some of the doctors who come to work in our practice have never come across rheumatic fever before because it's a Third World disease, virtually unknown in the UK and the US.

In the same way, I wouldn't know how to diagnose malaria: if someone came in with malaria I'd probably think they had the flu. But if I went and worked in another country, I should get informed about the health problems that are likely to occur there. If I was in Sierra Leone I should know about malaria. If I was in South Africa I should be on the lookout for AIDS. In New Zealand, doctors need to know about rheumatic fever and MRSA.

//

The system measures clinical competency. It says that our doctors should be able to recognise a set of symptoms and diagnose, investigate and treat those symptoms. If a diagnosis is incorrect we say that doctor is clinically incompetent and we review the matter to see if it's just acceptable human error or is grossly negligent, and we take disciplinary measures.

But we don't evaluate cultural competency; although if we did — if we asked what number of deaths occurred because of culturally incompetent care — I suspect we'd be shocked and dismayed. We need to incorporate cultural competency as a measure that our professional body signs up to and monitors and audits, with both training and disciplinary action available if necessary, just like we do with clinical competency.

So, a Māori patient comes in on five occasions over two years for gout and every time you see him, his blood pressure is sky high. Why not take the opportunity to put your cultural lens on? He's here for gout but we know that Māori rates of death from heart disease are 2.5 times higher than for Pākehā, and gout is a precursor for diabetes and heart disease. The first step is to ask him if he has a family history of heart disease.

'Oh yeah, my dad died at 40.'

'Now, what about your heart health . . . Oh, you're having chest pain?'

I challenge the health service: if a patient of mine gets rheumatic fever, why don't you come back and look at my notes and make sure I didn't see the child a month ago with a sore throat then gave them some paracetamol and sent them home, instead of giving them antibiotics and doing a throat swab? That's the way to audit my cultural competency.

'Lance, do a better job next time. Learn from that. We'll help you once, and then if it happens a second time we'll be more critical and ask why you didn't learn from that the first time.'

We doctors are smart, intelligent people. We can say, 'Thanks, you're right, I missed that. I want to learn from this and be a better doctor.'

//

There are many barriers to healthcare — socio-economic, cultural, geographic. With innovation and leadership we are doing our best to find ways of overcoming them.

Everyone loves the MOKO Programme, and now we have people outside our community of Kaitāia asking, How can you help us? These people live in Te Hapua or Te Kao, in Rangiātea or Karikari, too far away for our clinic staff to visit often, and yet they need our services.

On the bodies of young, Māori primary-school children we see eczema, we see open sores and infections on their arms and legs. This is how children are going to school, on a daily basis. Teachers often say: 'Do something about hakihaki — it's a more important problem than sore throats.' They say it's hard to teach kids, hard for kids to learn and to excel, if they've got a nasty sore on the back of their knee and it's ferociously itchy or acutely painful.

RHEUMATIC FEVER IS A THIRD WORLD DISEASE, VIRTUALLY UNKNOWN IN THE UK AND THE US.

Compared to other developed countries, New Zealand has one of the highest rates of serious skin infections, particularly among kids. Over the past decade, the number of children admitted to hospital for the treatment of serious skin infections has doubled, according to the Best Practice Advocacy Centre New Zealand. Māori and Pasifika families are most at risk, and it's getting worse, not better. From 1990 to 1999 Māori and Pacific children were, respectively, 2.3 and 3.7 times more likely to be admitted to hospital for a skin infection than children of other ethnicities. Between 2000 and 2007 this increased to 2.9 and 4.5 times, respectively. A report prepared for the Ministry of Health in 2012, 'Te Ohonga Ake: The Health Status of Māori Children and Young People in New Zealand', found that 'In New Zealand during 2006–2010, hospital admissions for serious skin infections were significantly higher for Māori than for non-Māori, non-Pacific children and young people.' The trend has continued upwards into 2013.

Skin infections are heavily influenced by socio-economic factors. During the period 1990–99 the rate of infection in children from New Zealand's most deprived areas was 3.6 times greater than for the wealthiest areas. Between 2000 and 2007 this ratio increased to 4.3. As the gap widens between those at the top of our socio-economic scale and those at the bottom, we can expect ever greater disparity in health outcomes, particularly in diseases associated with poverty such as skin infections, respiratory illnesses and rheumatic fever.

The idea that sores will just go away in time is wrong; we know, in fact, they can cause serious illness — skin infections are linked to kidney disease, rheumatic heart disease, and joint and bone damage.

So that was another issue that required a bit of leadership. We needed to look at something innovative. We asked the question: Does the patient always have to be sitting in front of the doctor to get the care they need?

Technology suggests they don't. In Kaitāia, if you have a sore shoulder and you need to see an orthopaedic surgeon, you have to drive two and a half hours to Whāngārei to be assessed for two minutes by a specialist who will tell you to come back next week for an MRI — that's another five-hour trip. But in our community we have an innovative physiotherapist who set up a video conference with the specialist in Whāngārei, with our physiotherapist moving the patient's shoulder into the right positions. Then, when the specialist says, 'You need to get an MRI,' it's one trip versus two.

I realised we could use technology in the same way to connect our clinic with remote communities. We could treat these kids in a non-traditional way with tele-medicine — medicine at a distance. We use smart devices and a specially designed app to capture information about the skin infection and send it back to the clinic, so I or a nurse can diagnose and prescribe treatment. Then I can send the medicine up to that community using rural delivery, and they will receive it the next day — much better than waiting a week for a doctor to visit. Much better than the family having to pay fuel costs for what might be a 120 kilometre round trip. Much better than the family not receiving any help, which is what often happens.

And if we treat these skin infections earlier, we won't have to admit these kids to hospital. Hospital costs around $1000 a day, and that's unaffordable for our health system. We believe the technology allows us to provide a health service that's smarter and cheaper and more effective than the current model.

We called this new programme vMOKO — 'virtual MOKO' — and it represents an important aspect of our practice: looking at different ways of delivering health to the most disadvantaged people. We're not waiting for somebody down in Wellington or the DHB to think up a solution to a problem; we're finding our own solutions.

Sure, we are chasing the taxpayer dollar like everyone else, where the government says what service they want to provide and we go and provide it. That's called the same old same old. But the government also has a small amount of funding — Whānau Ora's Whānau Integration, Innovation and Engagement Fund — for people who want to explore new possibilities, and that's where we want to be, in that space.

We have a number of contracts that are in that innovative space, receiving pilot funding to see if they'll work, and vMOKO is one of them. vMOKO is targeted specifically at high-needs Māori children to give them access to health services while they're at school. Schools are naturally community hubs. But another important point is that schools have very secure broadband access.

So often, services to these communities are ad hoc, not tailored to needs and conditions. vMOKO works because we, the health professionals, go into these communities and enlist local people into the scheme. It's a programme based on a partnership between health practitioners, the school and the parents and caregivers in the community.

To get people enlisted, the clinic sets up a meeting at the school where we talk to the parents and teachers. I tell them, 'I believe people like you are better at looking after your children than people like me.'

Then we explain how it works: we supply the school with digital scales, a digital thermometer and a digital pulse-meter. We also provide an iPad loaded with an application that allows them to record all the health information for each child, and to take photos of infections. Volunteers from the local community are then trained to use the equipment and collect information, which they send back to the clinic in Kaitāia for me to diagnose and treat.

The digital age gives us the opportunity to use technology to span the geographic gap, and to involve members of each community in the healthcare of their children. We bring the tools, then we step back. We're empowering people to look after themselves. Through technology, and some clinical tools, people can then care for their own families.

We hope this programme will, over time, bring greater health knowledge and literacy to these communities, along with the immediate health outcomes. So while treating children is one part of the programme, treating communities, educating communities and empowering communities is probably the greater part of what we're doing

Of course there are safeguards. If the child is normally a well child, and their temperature is OK, their pulse is OK and the parents have signed a consent form saying the kid doesn't have type 1 diabetes or an allergy to medication — then we can easily prescribe treatment without physically seeing the child. If the child has a temperature above a certain level, or their heart rate is not normal, the app simply will not let the volunteer go further; it gives the instruction that the child needs to see a doctor.

The underlying point is that the kids came to school with these sores that their parents thought were normal. What they think is normal is quite different from what really is normal. Skin infection is so common in the Far North that both caregivers and teachers have stopped seeing it as a problem. Therefore, part of our programme is to educate our communities to know when something is wrong.

This isn't a reflection on these people being bad parents or bad teachers — I just think our radar is down on these things. Also, there has been no other option until now; it's been too hard to see a doctor. But now, through our programme, the service comes to them, and all the antibiotics are free of charge, thanks to KidsCan. My generous friend Ray Stark from Talking Tech Foundation has donated the iPads and developed the app. He is a great partner and his support is invaluable. It's so incredibly encouraging to have other people say we're doing a good job and offering to help us. It's even great just to be patted on the shoulder. But when people like Julie Chapman from KidsCan and Ray Stark say they want to help and offer such incredible resourcing or funding, it is really awesome.

I honestly think that in 12 months we'll be taking vMOKO outside Northland, and maybe even outside New Zealand, as it has so many possibilities for remote communities everywhere. The values and principles behind the programme — particularly community empowerment and combating inequality — will strike a chord with indigenous peoples everywhere. Indigenous peoples around the world want the same things from their healthcare.

Tele-medicine is innovative, and that's a scary word for some people. It means change. It means doing things differently, trying a different approach, and if that doesn't work, trying something else. As long as we're doing it safely, I believe it has great potential for all my patients — adults as well as children.

14 // TAKING IT TO THE COMMUNITY

Much about success lies in tailoring the message to the people you want to help. The marae is a really important part of our community but mostly it is used for tangi and hui. Why don't we bring a health service that is effective, and professionals who are local and have relevance to marae? It's better speaking to a hui at a marae than speaking to one person in a doctor's room.

Speaking to groups works well in terms of my time. Imagine if I have 30 individual appointments and spend 15 minutes talking to each individual. On the marae I can spend an hour with 30 people, and can speak in more detail and be more inspiring.

As a people, we do everything together. Our lives are centred on whānau, and as whānau we need to support each other. This is the thinking behind our new quit-smoking programme — which we call Te Hātūturu.

Te Hātūturu means 'the original breath'. By giving the programme this name we are encouraging our people to return to a more traditional, authentic way of thinking. The breath in Māori culture is symbolically very important — it holds the lifeforce of the person; so when you hongi you press noses not to press noses but to exchange breath. That's the purpose of hongi: to mingle breath. You are connecting with that new person you've just met through this exchange of breath. When you hongi some people, you'll hear them breathing in deeply, ingesting you.

We're saying:

Consider your breath sacred, and therefore consider what comes out of it.

Consider smoking a cultural insult rather than just a physical insult.

Your journey to being smokefree is about cultural strength, rather than physical wellbeing.

I'm thinking we could use this approach for more than smoking — for diabetes, kidney failure. These different approaches don't cost much money but may be more effective. We have so much waste in our health system. In 2014, health received approximately $15 billion from the national budget. About one-fifth of this is spent on primary care, the area that has the biggest potential for reducing disease. The most expensive cost to our health system is hospital-level care, where we are responding to disease rather than preventing it. It is like buying more life boats for the *Titanic* rather than developing smarter ways to prevent it from sinking.

Smoking is a real problem for our people. In Northland, 34 per cent of Māori regularly smoke, compared with 16 per cent of non-Māori. Lung cancer and other smoking-related illnesses are leading causes of premature death. Māori kids under 15 are four times more likely to smoke than non-Māori; Māori adults, especially women, are twice as likely as non-Māori to smoke.

People feel very guilty about smoking, and guilt is part of the reason they don't come to the doctor.

I'd rather not go than feel a sense of shame and guilt.

I don't think it's intentional, but I've seen this guilt-trip attitude among some of the student doctors I have working with me. I was with one of them when he was checking a female patient who'd come in with a chesty cough and he immediately said to me, 'She's a smoker.' I watched this young student ask this woman how many she was smoking a day and when she said, 'One too many,' her head just went down. I could see she felt ashamed and embarrassed.

SMOKING IS A WESTERN DISEASE, BUT I HAVE A FEELING WE CAN USE OUR CULTURE TO HELP US STOP.

I know this patient really well, and I don't approach her smoking like that. Labelling someone a smoker is so dehumanising. Instead I put my hand on her shoulder and speak warmly to her. I say, 'Kia kaha, you've got to try to give up. I know how hard it is but, you know, when the time is right I'm going to support you, and you know it will be good for your breathing.'

We don't tell people enough about the reasons why they find it hard to give up: smoking is as addictive as heroin, and since birth they have been exposed to marketing strategies to get them hooked. New Zealand cigarettes have the second highest level of nicotine — the addictive bit — in the world, and the highest tar.

A patient said to me once he had grown up with a mother who smoked all the time. One of the reasons he smoked was because the smell of cigarette smoke reminded him of her. 'Give me something that will replace that feeling,' he said.

Two years later this same guy had a heart attack. He was 39. You might think heart attacks are the domain of a 60-year-old — maybe a 50-year-old; definitely not someone in their thirties. He survived that attack, but because he has now moved away I don't know whether he made the significant lifestyle changes he needed to in order to turn his health around.

We offer more than moral support when it comes to smoking. I prescribe medication to help people to stop: this is the most effective way to quit smoking. Cold turkey is about 15 per cent successful. Patches are about 20 per cent effective over a year. Medication is between 30 and 48 per cent effective. I'm a Western doctor. I believe drugs can help, and I feel very strongly that they are a tool I can use to help our people become smokefree.

But I also know drugs are just a tool. We need to give our whānau a new way of acting, too. At the moment, they smoke on the building site at smoko, they stand outside the kōhanga and smoke, they smoke with a cup of coffee after the kids are in bed. Western medicine runs strong in my veins. But manaaki aroha — loving care — also runs strongly through my veins. Smoking is a Western disease, but I have a feeling we can use our culture to help us stop.

It takes time, trial and error to become effective. But now we're in the process of establishing a new programme that takes a different approach. It's about going to the marae, where the people are, and trying to work with them at the community level.

//

Our first community meeting for Te Hātūturu was at Te Hāpua marae — New Zealand's northernmost settlement, and a community that has suffered greatly over the last 150 years. Smoking rates are high, but on the marae only a small number of people were gathered, and most of them were non-smokers. There was no point being disappointed at that turnout. Instead, it was an opportunity to reflect on *how* we do what we do. We want to be effective at working with whānau, so how can we do that?

Shifting the focus of where we deliver healthcare is a great start. But once we are physically in the community, how do we take that next step of meaningfully reaching into people's lives? The low turnout at Te Hāpua energised my thinking.

We could create health champions in family units. Say you've got a family unit which is 50 people directly and indirectly related to each other, living and moving in the same circles. Why don't we engage with and maybe employ a health champion who's charged with making sure everyone in that 50-person group has had those important preventive healthcare tests: immunisation, smoking cessation, smears, mammograms, heart checks, diabetes checks. That same person can be responsible for accident prevention in the family, through training and with some support.

There is so much relevance in a health champion who actually comes from that family unit, talking to their auntie or uncle, nephew or niece, asking if they've had this or that done.

We've got close to 3000 patients registered now with our practice. Maybe we'd start with 10 people, each with more than 20 people in their direct or indirect family, to trial the programme. These 10 would be interested in being a paid health champion, keen to take responsibility as the bridge between the health system and whānau.

At the moment, the doctors get funding if immunisation rates improve. What if we shifted some of that performance funding to the health champion? Say we get $10,000 a year if our immunisation rates are over 90 per cent. What if we said, it costs us $7000 to deliver an immunisation programme, but why don't we give $3000 to the health champions? If we also take some of our performance funding for heart and diabetes screening and mammograms and smears and smoking, pretty soon there's a big pot of money. Rather than keeping it for ourselves and patting ourselves on the back, we would be empowering that community to look after their own health, and to reap the many rewards of doing so.

We've thought about that before, and we could easily implement it in our practice. It would take a little bit of resourcing and support to do it, and a strong will and some innovation.

The health champion idea could really work for the anti-smoking campaign, to get our messages and the resources right inside the whānau in a way that's hard to do, even when we've come right to the marae in the heart of the community.

//

I'm not always the best person to deliver health messages. I forget that while in some ways I am like my patients, I have become unlike them: I'm highly educated, articulate, fit. I have a good income. I've had opportunities. If I go into a community and talk about an issue that I want them listen to, even though I'm Māori, there's a perception of difference.

Lance, we get $17 an hour. We're trying to feed our kids. It's hard going, we've got a lot of stresses.

Health messages work a lot better if they come from one of your own who has suffered from the diseases I'm talking about, rather than from me with my clinical knowledge but no personal experience.

One of the most powerful people I heard speaking about heart failure was dying because of his damaged heart. He said, 'Boys, listen to me. It's too late for me, but don't let it be too late for you.' It's really powerful stuff. This is a far more powerful message than I can deliver, and all the more powerful because he could say, 'I know how hard it is.' This was when I was involved in a programme called One Heart Many Lives. This programme was designed to encourage more Māori and Pasifika men to get their hearts checked. It was based on a concept called social marketing that uses marketing concepts alongside other approaches to influence behaviours that benefit individuals and communities for the greater social good. What I witnessed with this particular man was a potent message that was the most authentic health promotion I have ever seen. Here was a man who was a father, a husband, a brother, an uncle and a mate, who honestly told others in our group that his path was not one to follow. His words reached those in the room far more effectively than those of a well-intentioned Māori doctor would have.

Do I really know how hard it is to deal with 180 kilograms of body weight and high blood pressure and being told I should give up smoking, when it's such an addictive thing and it's been around me all my life? Do I really know how hard it is to be told I've got to manage my gout better and exercise more and stop eating all the food I was brought up on? I wasn't even brought up on boil-up.

Taking all this on board, I think when it comes to health promotion campaigns, we need to engage with local people, so that local people are talking to each other.

Every community is distinct. Our community is quite different from communities in Wellington or Auckland. So my idea is to get some local people who have suffered mental health issues or breast cancer or lung cancer, or diabetes with all its complications, and invite them to tell their story, which we could video and show on an iPad in our waiting room. They are the people whom others in their community can relate to and identify with.

My experience is that people love to tell their stories if they think it will help. Women with breast cancer often say, 'I don't want other women to go through what I went through.'

I had a patient, a local man, who'd hammered his heart from drinking, and I pushed him to get a heart transplant. In turn he became a powerful advocate for persuading men to look after their heart health. 'I made bad choices and my heart suffered but yours doesn't need to,' he would say. He actually had his old heart — it had been all sliced up for examination after the operation, but it was preserved — and he'd bring it along to meetings in a vacuum-packed bag.

Imagine holding your own heart. And, even more so, he shared how emotional he got when he thought about whose heart he now had beating inside him, because you never know who the donor is. And he talked about some of that responsibility he carried, of carrying someone's heart. Quite deep. Through him, I was able to witness the power of getting your patients engaged in the process of educating the broader community.

He had his new heart for five years before he died, but he was able to reach many Māori men with his message of the importance of looking after your heart.

I love the idea that people could be sitting in our waiting room, looking at the videos on an iPad, connecting with the stories of others who have had the same health issues.

//

What we are talking about is health literacy, and while there is much to be gained from people sharing their experiences of and insights into illness, there is of course a real need for doctors to get better at passing on information about health.

The old saying that knowledge is power is so true in the delicate environment of health. Examples of miscommunication leading to tragic outcomes are all too common. A very common instance is the middle-aged man who sits at home having a heart attack and perhaps dying because he doesn't recognise that the squeezing feeling he's experiencing across his chest is what the doctor would call 'angina' and is a symptom of coronary disease.

Another example is the young mum whose child has a high temperature and rash. She doesn't think it's serious because she's waiting for the more well-known sign of neck stiffness before going to the doctor. She simply doesn't know that a high temperature and a rash means she should ring her doctor immediately.

The idea of health literacy is to break down very complex health information in a way that makes sense to everyday people. I often listen to medical students telling me in the most technical and complicated terms they can find, the reason for a patient's visit and what they plan to do with the patient. What must it feel like to be the subject of such an important discussion but not know what the heck is being said? I think we may as well be speaking Xhosa, or talking underwater, for all the patient can understand.

The same thing happens on the wards at the hospital. A high-powered team of three or more doctors, as many nurses, a charge nurse and a physiotherapist all stand at the end of the bed, conferring with each other about all the likely possibilities contributing to the patient's unfortunate state.

Lack of knowledge is a barrier to a positive healthcare experience — but just as important is the manner in which information is delivered. Of course, the type of information a patient can digest is dependent on things such as their education, health experience (both personal and wider family), self-esteem and confidence, and the comfort of the environment they are in at the time. I constantly challenge my student doctors to ensure that the patient is more aware of their condition when they leave our rooms than they were when they came in. This has the potential to save lives and improve patients' experiences.

//

Fifty per cent of what we do in healthcare is about trying to change people's behaviour, whether it's encouraging a better diet and more exercise, or getting them to stop smoking. We under-resource the support for behaviour change.

We're good at finding out what medication you need but we're very poor at engaging you and inspiring you to take it. Doctors have, on average, 15-minute consultations. We'll spend 10 minutes diagnosing and contemplating diagnostic algorithms about what treatment you need, then we'll take a couple of minutes to rattle off the name of the drug we're prescribing and to explain the side-effects and so on — and that leaves about 30 seconds to encourage you to actually take it.

It's that final step that we don't have a lot of skill or time for. What happens in between that moment of receiving the prescription, and the moment when the patient either does or doesn't actually take the drug as prescribed? What governs their behaviour? Why do some patients not follow through and take their medicine — or even take their prescription to the pharmacy? Instead of asking these questions, we tend to be quite judgemental: *You haven't taken your medicine and that's not good.*

In our clinics we have doctors and nurses, but we don't have a behavioural specialist. Doctors are taught very little about behaviour modification, and although it's such a central part of our work we fall into it by chance and not by design. An ideal workforce would have a significant number of staff skilled in that area; in particular, for us, someone who could put it in a Māori framework.

Medical practice is not about just writing prescriptions — it's so much more about relations with families and communities, and the magic bullet of changing behaviour.

KI TE KĀHORE HE WHAKAKITENGA KA NGARO TE IWI

//

WITHOUT FORESIGHT OR VISION THE PEOPLE WILL BE LOST

— KĪNGI TĀWHIAO PŌTATAU TE WHEROWHERO

PART 4 //

—
LEADERSHIP

15 // THE MOKO FOUNDATION

The MOKO Foundation is our registered charitable trust, set up to change the world, starting with the Far North of New Zealand.

I have a patient, a wonderful young boy. He had terrible eczema on his face — it was so bad he'd been hiding in his bedroom for six months; hadn't been to school, hadn't been learning. All he needed was to be seen by a dermatologist. We tried to get him an appointment through the public health system. You know how long it would have taken? Six months. So I said, bugger that, and we used our foundation money. It cost about $1000 altogether to get him and a caregiver down to Auckland, an appointment with the specialist, a night in a motel and a trip to Rainbow's End. The money had all been donated and I had no qualms about using it. It was the right thing for this kid.

But it was all too little too late for this boy. Most people don't know this, but treating such bad eczema can lead to blindness, and that's what happened to him. The treatment caused the formation of cataracts. He had eye surgery at

Greenlane to correct those, but there were complications and his lens was damaged.

When he comes to see me in my office, his mother has to hold his hand so he can make it from the chair to the door. He has been unable to attend school and I am worried about the impact this may have on his future.

//

Tracy and I established the MOKO Foundation in 2013. We wanted to separate our commercial business from our charitable aspirations. It has five trustees: me and Tracy, Brendon Morrissey (the principal of decile 1 Kaitāia Primary), a local detective who's also a prominent church leader, and a family lawyer who works a lot with the same sort of people we work with.

WE WANT TO SUPPORT THOSE WHO ARE ALREADY DOING THE WORK WITH VULNERABLE PEOPLE, AND VULNERABLE CHILDREN IN PARTICULAR.

Our work among vulnerable children and communities had sparked incredible support from mainstream New Zealand, and increasingly we were being sent cheques by people who wanted to help us. One woman sent a very large donation because she supported the notion that all people deserve access to quality healthcare and cost should not be a barrier. That was an amazing kickstart and an invaluable pat on the back. It's really encouraging for me as a Māori doctor, a Māori champion for our people in the Far North, that someone in Auckland, who looks quite different from me and comes from a different background, says, *That's not right*, and supports what we're doing.

Our aim is to put a percentage of the profits from our commercial business into the foundation. We do this unofficially anyway, with a whole lot of things, but we want to formalise that in the long term. So with that money and other money from some people who give on a regular basis, we created this foundation. It has three main focuses: health, education and leadership.

We want to support those who are already doing the work with vulnerable people, and vulnerable children in particular. Could they be helped by a $2000 or $3000 grant, or could we provide some kind of medical assistance? For instance, there's a small group of women, church-based, who provide after-school care for kids from a local primary. They feed these children and give them some tuition. How is that anything but fantastic? I mean, that's New Zealander of the Year territory, that is. I can go to them and say, 'You're doing a great job, how can we help? How can we be a link between you and some other funders?'

That's the beauty of my winning these awards: funders are looking at us and we have access to people and resources that we can commandeer on behalf of others for the community's benefit. For instance, we are hoping to form relationships with large, philanthropic organisations. I say to these organisations: 'We feel we're a safe pair of hands for the good work that you want to do, but you may not have the reach in the community that we have. What about using us as an intermediary — we can see your intentions through, but with a better local knowledge.'

These are some of the things were doing. In partnership with our local pharmacist, we can pay for prescriptions for people who otherwise wouldn't be able to afford them. We have an emergency fund to get people to see a specialist, and we've used it to help several kids get down to Auckland to see specialists when the wait for a hospital appointment was just too long.

//

It's a tough one. We are spending private funds on what is really core business for the DHB or the Ministry of Health. But on the other hand we are helping vulnerable people who can't afford to spend $300 to see a private specialist. So, in desperate situations, we've had to fill that gap. We've shown leadership. We just go off and do it, and, because our pockets are lined by the generosity of other New Zealanders, thank goodness we are able to.

But we shouldn't have to.

As I've discussed in chapter 13, we have huge, huge problems with skin-related diseases in Northland, yet our kids can't see a dermatologist because the DHBs only have a certain amount of money set aside for dermatology. Unbelievable. You'd cry at the state in which some of these kids come to see me.

So, I've formed a relationship with a private dermatologist in Auckland who has been incredibly generous and supportive of our desire to help these children. We work together using digital technology. I take photos of the skin conditions on my phone, and send her the photos. Imagine if I had a proper virtual clinic set up, with proper lighting and a proper high-definition camera. We've now worked together on about a dozen cases and had great outcomes.

In one case I had a young baby with a really bizarre rash. I didn't know what it was. The child had been seen by two or three doctors and then a specialist doctor, and no one had been able to help. All treatment had failed. I took one photo on my iPhone and sent it down to the dermatologist. She quickly got back to me. 'It could be condition X,' she said. 'It's very rare, but it means that Mum has condition Y, so test Mum and if condition Y shows up we'll know what to do.'

She was right on the money. The child had a condition which reflected a problem the mother had. We treated and continue to monitor the mother, and the child got better. That was the first time I have ever diagnosed a condition in a patient who was not my principal patient — and it was all because of a photo.

I'm certain I am going to have a very good outcome from our work with tele-medicine, and with our trialling of vMOKO. I would like to show the funders that we could get more bang for our buck by utilising a tele-medicine approach for dermatology cases in vulnerable communities.

//

Through the foundation we also look at the environments people live in. I know that giving people a prescription for an asthma attack or skin infection and sending them home to run-down houses that are cold and damp is like pouring money into a hole in the ground, or using a finger to plug a hole in a dyke. More importantly, it's a missed opportunity for improved health outcomes. So we set up Kainga Ora, a programme to fix run-down homes, because wellness begins in warm, safe homes.

I went around the community and when I came across a home that looked unhealthy I knocked on the door and introduced myself. 'I'm a local doctor and I'm just playing with this idea that unhealthy homes could be contributing to the poor health of the people living in them. Could I come in and have a look? And could you talk to me about your health needs?'

Some people warned me I'd get doors closed in my face, but it was quite the opposite. People wanted to show me.

We decided to tackle a number of homes, shifting them from being unhealthy to healthy, and so improving the health of the families living in them. The idea was three homes each year. In one home we found a family of five kids and their grandmother who were so cold they had their oven turned up to high and the door open. They didn't use two of the bedrooms because they were damaged by leaks, by domestic violence and disrepair. No prescription medication was going to fix the health of this family.

A building company from Hamilton donated a brand-new roof, and we all got stuck in. Conor, our eldest son, and I and another student doctor helped put on the roof, and Talking Tech Foundation donated a new hot-water cylinder because the old one was leaking so badly. That was probably the most successful health outcome I achieved in eight or nine years practising in Kaitāia.

We worked on three houses. But to be really successful, this scheme requires the coordination of services and more funding than we have. We are working to put together a team of people to make the assessments and plan for the repairs. We need community groups to volunteer their labour, and organisations to offer supplies and materials. We are currently trying to formalise something to get this working. This is true doctoring — a way of getting more bang for the health buck.

A healthy environment is the most potent intervention we can give some of these families with recurrent illnesses. It's fair to say that out of everything I could possibly achieve, creating warm, safe homes for children would be the most effective.

//

The MOKO Foundation offers a scholarship in honour of my dear friend Hawea Vercoe, a great young Māori leader who tragically died in 2009. At just 36, Hawea had achieved so much and was recognised as someone at the forefront of Māori leadership. His many roles in the community included being principal of Te Kura Kaupapa Māori o Rotoiti, a member of the Rotorua District Council's Te Arawa standing committee and a councillor of what is now known as the Bay of Plenty Regional Council. We felt that his contribution shouldn't die with him, and so we created the Hawea Vercoe Leaders Scholarship, available to Year 12 and 13 students with a passion for Māori culture and who want to reach their leadership potential. Our inaugural 2014 scholar is an incredible young man who is already a leader at 16. Ezekiel Raui's ambition is nothing less than to be the first Māori prime minister, via the legal profession. I can't help him on his pathway to law, but I can mentor him for the year, show him leadership in action, and introduce him to Māori District Court judge Greg Davis, who can support his aspirations. With my contacts and profile I can open doors for others.

My hope is that in five years' time we'll have 50 or 100 Hawea Vercoe Leaders Scholarship mentors, keen to be part of our vision, who believe that the pathway to leadership for Māori youth should happen by design and not by chance.

My own pathway to leadership was through chance, and I always wonder what might have happened if, from about the age of 17, I'd been mentored by someone who sat with me every month and talked to me about my goals and dreams.

In 2014 we gave 24 MOKO Awards across nine schools — primary, intermediate and secondary — to kids who are making the right decisions. They might not be the ones who are top of the class, but they continually demonstrate a great sense of community spirit, they have aspirations and they do their best. We give $500 to kids going on to tertiary education or trade training, $250 to kids still at high school, $100 to those at intermediate, and $50 to those at primary school. The money helps to buy textbooks or stationery or whatever that child needs; plus the award gives them encouragement. The kids are nominated by the school principals. These awards were designed to go to students who are hovering between mediocrity and greatness. With a push, they might 'fall' into greatness.

IN 2014 WE GAVE 24 MOKO AWARDS ACROSS NINE SCHOOLS TO KIDS WHO ARE MAKING THE RIGHT DECISIONS.

Here are some examples of the praise for these great kids.

'The characteristics that stand out in this student are not just her academic abilities but her honesty and caring nature. She helps those who need it the most. She is very independent and knows right from wrong. She is deserving of this award for the compassion she has towards her peers.'

'This student comes to school every day with the right attitude for learning. She is always looking out for the welfare of others and will put this above her own needs.'

'This student wants to train in carpentry next year. He is a hard-working boy, a middle-of-the-road student. Hard family background, but has kept coming and working. He has a leadership role in the whānau group, and assisted with the tuakana-teina programme [a mentoring programme for learning te reo]. Has a strong caring streak, and is self-motivated and conscientious.'

'This hard-working student is heading to university next year. She has achieved merits in Level 1, 2 and likely Level 3. Involved heavily in senior leadership and school community, including whānau group. There will be financial struggles for her next year.'

These are the extraordinary ones, those who are achieving despite all the pressures in their lives.

16 // NO GUILT, NO GRIEVANCE

I was in my second or third year at medical school when Lion Breweries did an ad campaign for their Lion Red beer, featuring single words that they felt captured the essence of their product, like pride, family, mates. White words on a red background. One of the words they used was mana, and when I saw it up there on a billboard I thought, *That's not right.*

Mana is a word that talks about strength, pride and honour. It's a Māori word, almost the ultimate Māori word, and of course I knew the association between Māori culture and alcohol — especially high-volume, cheap alcohol like Lion Red.

So I went down to Lion Breweries' headquarters on Khyber Pass near Newmarket, in Auckland, and saw a woman already standing outside the gate.

'Are you protesting about the mana thing?'

She was, so we made a sign and we spent the afternoon protesting. All these cars were tooting at us. Māori would drive past going, 'Yeah, tino pai!', then Pākehā would drive past and go, 'Get a job!' We got interviewed on TV and radio. In the end a manager from Lion Breweries came down and said, 'I understand', and they removed the word mana from their ad campaign.

//

The way forward for us as a nation is without guilt or grievance. I say this whether I'm talking to Māori or mainstream audiences, and I think both groups need to hear it. In saying that, it's important to note that I've been on a journey myself in regard to my feelings about the treatment of Māori, and our status in New Zealand society. I have been angry, and there was a time when I felt that for Māori no good has ever come from European arrival. This was a personal space in which anger, resentment and grievance were strong, and I'm really proud of the fact that I've moved to a different place now.

WE ARE NOT ANTI-PĀKEHĀ. WE ARE PRO-MĀORI.

Motivated by a sense of unfairness, Tracy and I became quite radical in our thinking. It's an easy path to take. Tracy's journey echoed my own. When I was a medical student we had the opportunity, through MAPAS, to go to marae where we'd meet other Māori doctors and become informed about the issues and statistics in their communities. They were all very passionate, borderline radical, pushing Māori health, talking about inequality. We'd sit at these hui — Tracy would be there, too — and listen and our eyes would be big, and we'd think: *That's not fair! That's not on!* It became a strongly shared thing between us.

We went to Waitangi. We marched with our flags on hīkoi to Wellington. We sent our kids to kōhanga and kura, and we protested and really pushed for Māori. But in recent years we've probably come back a bit, because you fight a lot in that space. There's a lot of anger going on and I don't think you can sustain that and get far. Whereas, coming back a little, we've been able to make a bit more progress, especially with what we're doing in our company and in our practice and in our network of relationships. You can't be too radical, or you scare people away.

We are not anti-Pākehā. We are pro-Māori. We are trying to find ways forward for our people. It's about being an advocate and, in a quiet way, a protester — but now we protest by getting out and doing the work, challenging our colleagues and challenging the health system.

I think a lot of our people are in that negative space of resentment, prejudice and grievance without being fully aware of it. They carry it without naming it. They probably don't sit down and think, 'I am having some very strong anti-Pākehā sentiments, but I'm comfortable with that, or I'm uncomfortable with that and I'm trying to change it.' I think people just go, 'I don't like her, and I don't like him.' It's to do with consciousness. If you have those negative feelings and you're not even aware of what they are, they transform into resentment and anger, or into a kind of hopeless apathy. There's no positive outlet for them.

I'm trying to get my people to see the value in letting some things go for their own benefit — not because it's going to make the other party feel better, but because grievance just holds you back. It's like when someone has been the victim of a crime: to heal and move on they need to let go of a bit of the hurt.

It is reasonable and justified to be politically aware of the historical issues, to see the relationship between colonisation and the current state of my people, and the apathy or prejudice or racism that results in the horrific statistics that I see the evidence of every day. But for me it's been important to focus my energy away from grievance and into a different space where I acknowledge that things have occurred but now I look at how we can progress: How do we bring other people on board for our cause? How do we learn to open up and say, 'We're struggling and we need your help to advance our cause'?

My transition out of anger and resentment has been happening over the last few years, but in the last 24 months it's been accelerated by the fact that some of my greatest supporters are Pākehā. This has been a very interesting revelation — that non-Māori New Zealanders believe that what we're doing in a community like the Far North is important to all New Zealanders.

And so I believe that fringe politics is not the way forward for Māori.

//

Because of my background and training, I am comfortable in both worlds, Māori and Pākehā. I have the opportunity to be a bridge between groups. I have the respect of the mainstream because I have a medical, professional qualification; and I can command the respect of my people because I am kanohi kitea — the face that is seen. Kanohi kitea means *I'm present*. I'm not sitting in an ivory tower in a university or in the halls of power in Wellington. I'm a person on the ground, advocating for Māori.

There is no benefit to be gained from guilt and fear. If I feel guilty about something I've done, nothing positive comes out of that; I just feel stink. It's a feeling that goes nowhere.

When I was younger and listening to the teachings of some of the more radical people in the Māori movement, I would go, *Yeah this is right . . . This is wrong . . . We've got to fight it. We've got to make them feel guilty and make them change things.* But the reality is we will wait a long time for that to happen if we create conflict and choose confrontation. There is more to be gained from getting people on board.

But we can't forget the past; the past is a part of who we are and where we're heading. There are parts of our history that are holding us back, and the reason I'm seeing a whole lot of sick kids in Kaitāia today is because we've got a race of people coming back from the brink of extinction.

//

At the beginning of the twentieth century the Māori population was down to 42,000, almost obliterated by disease, famine and warfare. But Māori survived and are now almost 600,000-strong. That shows an incredible resilience. There's no doubt colonisation was brutal, and when I was younger, around 19 and 20, I was pretty angry. I did a lot of reading, and I was very disturbed by what I found out. I read about Gustavus von Tempsky, glorified by the colonials, who as one of the notorious Forest Rangers was renowned for riding through the forest with his long, curved sword, hacking at women and children as they ran from his path. There are many other examples. The colonial relationship was definitely not a match made in heaven, nor was it peaceful, subtle — or without consequences.

Colonisation has had an effect on Māori — loss of land and language are just the starting points. But we've been resilient enough to survive and rebuild. However, the last 100 years or so have seen a terrible apathy take hold of our country and its treatment of its indigenous people. Māori earn far less, are less likely to be educated, more likely to be incarcerated and more likely to die prematurely. That's because of apathy, not an active process or design. These things happen. We accept them. Everyone seems to accept them. That's the next level of brutality that we've faced as a result of colonisation, and it's as much a part of the historical process as von Tempsky's sword.

I often say to my own people: 'You are survivors, you are resilient, you are taonga — treasures that have been passed down. We have to look at how and where we apply our resilience now.'

//

A large part of the challenge in my work is trying to get our people to understand that in some ways they do have a lot of individual responsibility — that they can try to free themselves from the shackles of colonisation, of poverty and lack of spirit, all those things that hold them back. We can't just wait around and expect all our problems to magically get better.

Māori are still waiting for things to happen to them; and meanwhile there are Pākehā who believe we get too much favouritism and special treatment.

When I give presentations to both mainstream and Māori audiences, I often use pictures of some of the kids I see in my practice — and these pictures articulate the issues that drive me. These are sick children. Too many of these children die prematurely.

I don't think anybody in my audiences would think that's reasonable or something to be proud of. And I want every single person in my audience to know they can take part in changing that.

Pākehā wrestle a lot with this question of guilt. Even in my own family we've had discussions around the table with Pākehā friends and family, and some of them get very defensive because they feel they're being held liable or accountable for the actions of others, a long time ago. I've even had people say, really blatantly, 'I've got nothing to be guilty about. You've got it wrong, Lance. These guys are just lazy.'

There's a lot of fear around this subject — fear of losing something that they think they're entitled to; losing something that they fear they can't give up, when they probably could. Fear breeds prejudice. But why would you be fearful of better access to health services or healthy homes for children? Who can ever be afraid of children? I show these images of little beings who are full of potential and I say: *You can be a part of that.*

The way forward is without guilt or grievance.

In my own case, I had a chip on my shoulder because of my experiences growing up — my absent, alcoholic father; the 'isms': racism, classism and sexism that we saw targeted towards us and our solo, Pākehā mother raising half-caste kids on a benefit. But I have grown my strength from these 'disadvantages', rather than making them something I've built grievance on. I celebrate the fact that I found a very important part of who I am, which is Māori, and I display that with pride but also in an inclusive way.

My story is a microcosm of the story of my people. We acknowledge the past. We acknowledge the effects of that past on our lives today, and we look for positive ways to step forward.

We can celebrate the more than 50 settlements made under the Treaty of Waitangi. These settlements mean there's a chapter of our country's history that has been recognised, has been addressed, and is part of moving on.

//

I look forward to the time when all New Zealanders are engaged and involved in my culture. That is something we as Māori could push a lot more, and support others to learn more about. Imagine walking into a shop where you're greeted by 'Kia ora. E pēhea ana koe?' And you respond easily in te reo, and it would not be something weird but something cool: 'Kia ora. E pai ana ahau.' Sharing te reo would create links and identity; it would be about us being able to identify as Kiwi. At the moment we celebrate Māori culture in very restricted or limited situations, and we're a bit selective, too.

——

THERE ARE GROUPS WITH AGENDAS THAT WOULD SERVE TO KEEP MĀORI AND PĀKEHĀ APART RATHER THAN BRINGING US TOGETHER.

Tracy and I took all seven of our kids, as well as the little boy we look after, to watch the All Blacks at Eden Park in Auckland. The national anthem began, first in Māori, and it was sung with, say, 60 per cent energy from the crowd. Then we heard the national anthem in English and it was sung with 100 per cent energy. Then there was a breathtaking silence as the haka was performed, and at the end of it, 38,500 people threw their hands in the air, applauding and whistling, and there was this massive chorus of pride. My son Conor, who is 21, turned to me and said: 'Dad, what's up with that? Is it just that people don't know our national anthem in Māori that they don't have that same gusto, or is something else going on?'

He's right — there was a marked contrast between the pride in the haka with its fierce challenge, and the national anthem being sung in Māori. I bear in mind that it was only in 1999 at the opening of a Rugby World Cup match at Twickenham that soprano Hinewehi Mohi sang it for the first time in Māori — and there was an uproar. Since then it has become the custom to sing both versions. However, in South Africa, which has come through a far greater trial in terms of race relations, people can actually sing, with equal gusto, their anthem in Swahili and then Afrikaans and then English, in recognition of their diverse background.

In the case of the anthem and the haka, I don't think it's because they are different types of entertainment — one's boring and one's exciting — because we see the pride coming through when the anthem's sung in English. There is a certain level of discomfort around the Māori version of the national anthem. It's noticeable to Māori. Through the Māori lens, it's what we pick up. It's the difference between being the audience of a spectacle and being a participant.

There are people who would and could push our peoples apart. There are groups with agendas that would serve to keep Māori and Pākehā apart rather than bringing us together, and I think we have to recognise this and be cautious. Māori sometimes operate in a very hostile environment, whether we are trying to advocate for funding or for a particular policy change. I've sat in meetings about health conditions that affect 99.9 per cent Māori or Pasifika people and all of the experts at the table have been Pākehā. Māori and Pasifika people sit quietly at the back and don't feel they can enter that space to contribute in a really meaningful way. We need to be at the front of the solutions, not bystanders and spectators.

We've had a century and a half of sitting at the back of the classroom. Language was smacked out of us, and trades were our destiny. It's only been in very recent years that high numbers of us have entered tertiary education and begun to move in significant numbers into decision-making positions within the mainstream. Many Māori still feel very shy about taking their place at the table and voicing their own point of view.

I can see this happening in my own practice and profession, where if you think you have the knowledge you tend to dominate the conversation. I know that. I've gone into meetings where I thought I could tell a group of Māori men about men's health, because I'm a Māori man and I'm a doctor, but actually I needed to sit down and listen more than I talked. I think it's a complication of the academic and intellectual pedigree we think we have. It traps us in our own high opinion of ourselves and we forget there may be other perspectives.

The relationship between all this and my son's observation at the All Blacks game about the very different levels of enthusiasm shown for the national anthem in Māori and the haka is this: the acceptance of Māori culture by the mainstream is on the mainstream's terms. We might have a hongi and a hāngi to welcome a visiting world leader. But we don't take the step of, say, incorporating te reo Māori across the curriculum in the country. We won't make it compulsory because that's a swear word for people who think we're becoming a nanny state.

But I say let's embrace and share te reo with all of New Zealand so that when you're overseas you're recognised as a Kiwi because of your language which is unique to you, Pākehā and Māori. Māori culture will identify us all as Kiwi New Zealanders. I've had many amazing discussions with Pākehā New Zealanders who want to do just that.

17 // HEALTH WARRIOR

How do we encourage our patients to look after their
health? It's simple. You become a good role model to your
patients, live a healthy lifestyle. Walk the talk! You can't
expect your whānau and people to change their lifestyles
if you're not doing it yourself! I'm so proud of all our
kaimahi Te Kōhanga Whakaora who believe in keeping
active, live healthy lives and are all smokefree.
— Hinerangi Waikai, practice manager at Te Kōhanga
   Whakaora

After I was so humiliated by my father's drinking and offensive
behaviour at the indigenous doctors conference in Australia I
gave up drinking.

I did it because my father's alcoholic. I did it because I
saw the damage alcohol caused in our community. I did it
because I saw drinking happening in inappropriate settings
in my profession. I did it because I don't want to be a part-time
warrior for my people.

I didn't stop drinking because I was worried about getting

drunk and beating my wife up. I didn't stop drinking because I was worried about ruining my liver or crashing a car or getting locked up, or any of the other harm associated with hazardous drinking. I stopped drinking because of leadership. And, honestly, it was a conversation starter. I'd be at an event and have a glass of orange juice in my hand.

'Don't you drink?'

'No.'

'Why?'

'Well, if you've got 20 minutes I'll tell you . . .'

Taking a stand generates discussion and it encourages other people to think about it. I was making a point.

We had spent that conference discussing the effects of colonisation on our peoples, and the devastating social impacts of being poor — such as substance abuse. On the last night, as is usual at most conferences, there was a piss-up. And I was sitting there thinking, *This is weird. We've just had four days of hearing about the effects of colonisation on indigenous peoples and you guys are embracing this whole colonising behaviour*. Not only that, but my father was there, obnoxiously drunk, exhibiting all the destructiveness of those influences.

At these conferences, I believe we get into what you might call a zone, a learning mode, a spiritual level around really important and deep issues, and there's a process by which you go into and come out of that zone. I thought we desecrated that with very inappropriate behaviour. So after the conference I researched and wrote up a paper on alcohol and Māori, and the effects on indigenous communities around the world, but especially in New Zealand.

Before Europeans arrived, Māori society was one of the few in the world that did not use intoxicants. There was no local equivalent of tobacco, alcohol or recreational drugs. In fact, our tūpuna gave their own name to alcohol: waipiro, or stinking water. Māori, like many other indigenous peoples, have been decimated by the pervasive nature of waipiro. You do not need to look far to see the impact alcohol has had on our people. It is a major contributor to domestic violence, criminal behaviour, poverty, broken whānau and appalling health statistics. Today, Māori have four times the alcohol-related mortality of non-Māori, and more than double the rate of years of life lost due to alcohol.

I STOPPED DRINKING BECAUSE OF LEADERSHIP. AND, HONESTLY, IT WAS A CONVERSATION STARTER.

Waipiro took hold of our people at a time when our culture was being undermined; that is when concepts such as mana whenua, te reo, wairuatanga, tikanga and whanaungatanga were being eroded by the onset of colonisation. Our tūpuna realised the clear and present danger of waipiro to the health and wellbeing, the spirituality and the way of life of our people. Kīngi Tāwhiao, Te Puea, Te Whiti, Te Kooti, Rua Kēnana, Māui Pōmare, Te Rangi Hīroa (Sir Peter Buck) and Āpirana Ngata attempted to stem the tide of waipiro that was sweeping through our communities.

Many Māori leaders took steps to prevent its spread and use. Some hapū declared their community or marae dry, or at least they created strict controls around liquor. The King Country under Ngāti Maniapoto was declared a dry area in 1884. In the late nineteenth and early twentieth centuries, some Māori joined the prohibition movement.

An 1874 petition to Parliament by Whanganui Māori stated, '[Liquor] impoverishes us; our children are not born healthy because the parents drink to excess, and the child suffers; it muddles men's brains, and they in ignorance sign important documents, and get into trouble thereby; grog also turns the intelligent men of the Maori race into fools . . . grog is the cause of various diseases which afflict us. We are also liable to accidents, such as tumbling off horses and falling into the water; these things occur through drunkenness. It also leads on men to take improper liberties with other people's wives.'

In the early twentieth century the first crop of Māori doctors described drinking as a major social problem. Now we are in the twenty-first century, the evidence is all around us, and we are still saying the same things: alcohol is a cultural insult to our people, and one with devastating health implications. It really is no secret. The Ministry of Health states it quite categorically: 'The health burden of alcohol falls inequitably on Māori.'

So I presented my paper to our Māori doctors conference and to a young Māori leaders conference, and I issued a challenge — that we have alcohol-free conferences. I said, 'I want to challenge ourselves, I want to challenge us, I want to challenge you. We have young students here seeing us drinking, and it's wrong. Why can't we have a conference without alcohol?'

I explained that I found it distressing to be part of something good like this but where we also had this alcohol scene and so many people got toasted. It happens all around our culture — tangi and hui always finish off with drinking. Watch *Once Were Warriors* — that's our people. But, I said, we're leaders in our communities and we know how harmful alcohol is among our people.

My challenge was rejected.

They thought I was a nutter. They argued against it — these were senior academic people, and radical people who talk about racism and our people's health, and they were saying, 'Oh well, we've got to go through a process.'

It's bullshit.

You're the leaders; you make an executive decision.

It never happened.

If Māori doctors truly took a stand against alcohol, maybe Māori teachers and Māori lawyers might follow. We need leadership on this issue, and we need role-modelling.

That's why I stopped drinking altogether for the next eight years.

These days I very occasionally have a beer. I rarely if ever drink in public — that's partly because I don't want to lose my edge if I'm going to give a speech. But mostly the reason is that I think it's good to be a non-drinker. If I'm around people and I drink a little alcohol, not even getting drunk, I will not be remembered for that because it's not out of the ordinary. But if I'm not drinking, that is sometimes noticed and remembered.

//

Alcohol was why Mum left my dad. Alcohol abuse was what caused him to make decisions that were really poor, both when he was sober and when he was drunk. It caused him to have catastrophic health problems. It caused a massive dent in our lives.

In alcohol we have this thing that we think is really great — it socially lubricates people to be more free and comfortable. Yet it causes so much harm. Immeasurable harm really, across all sectors: justice, health, productivity, the economy, families and culture. I have had more experiences than I care to remember patching up people from the results of a drunken rage or from a car accident. Ask any police officer, fireman or ambulance officer and I believe they will say the same thing — alcohol-fuelled carnage is the biggest drug problem we have in New Zealand.

We tinker around at the bottom end — like changing the amount a person's allowed to drink if they're going to drive. We don't do enough to address the upstream causes. If we really wanted to make a change in the way our society uses alcohol, we would address the alcohol industry, honestly and upfront. We would say: 'We're going to make decisions that will be independent of your influence' — because the alcohol industry is a big driving factor in how we drink. It has an enormous impact through the presence of alcohol in supermarkets and in sponsorship, not to mention the ballooning of bottle stores in our communities. Wouldn't it make a positive difference on communities such as Glen Innes or Ōtāhuhu if kids and adults didn't have to walk past liquor stores containing pallets of cheap alcohol, stacked up, 10 boxes high, right on the corner of the road, often near their schools?

Low-strength, high-volume alcohol (e.g. beer and RTDs) at a low cost is a recipe only for disaster. The answer is to tax alcohol at a much higher rate: put the price up. This would be a more accurate reflection of the cost of the industry to society. And it would bring alcohol back to being a privilege and a treat, rather than an everyday event. That measure alone would discourage high-volume drinking. And we know that would decrease family violence. Tobacco control measures recently implemented show that you can influence people's behaviour through taxes. I see patients on a regular basis who want to stop smoking because of the cost. We could do the same for alcohol.

Some people say doing any of these things would just drive alcohol underground; but that's the industry justifying their position. I would say that they are worried their sales are at risk.

I count the cost of this industry every day. Here's one example out of the endless cases I see: I had a woman in my clinic recently who had been abused by the men in her life from a young age. It began when she was a child; alcohol dulled her parents' sense of responsibility and care so that one of their friends — an 'uncle' who had also probably been drinking — could easily come into her bed. Almost every partner she'd had abused alcohol. She herself acknowledges she's an alcoholic. I have many patients who tell me about how, as kids, they just hated parties because they knew that's when these guys would come into their beds.

Anyway, if you were to put a dollar amount on the harm done to this particular woman it would be well over $1 million. She's been on welfare forever. She's had nine kids, some of whom have been cared for through CYF. She's had relationships with a series of men who have treated her badly. She has post-traumatic stress syndrome and depression. Some of her children have in turn also been abused and they are now having children, so they're dysfunctional, and this cycle is creating another generation of costly, dysfunctional families.

She's a smart, strong woman. Imagine the life she could have had. She never had a chance. Alcohol is a driving factor in how her life has turned out.

When patients like this come to see me I know that my job has to be about more than just what happens in the clinic — the prescriptions, the bandages, taking blood pressure. Some days I get sprained ankles and chesty coughs and sore throats and these things are a blessing and a relief because I can easily fix them. But the social issues behind the ailments a patient presents with — the cold homes, the alcohol abuse, all the social problems that come with poor communities — these are the things that are incredibly difficult to treat with pills and medication that I can prescribe.

//

I used to drive my car to work every day. Then one day I noticed this older guy biking along the road. I knew him — he's the bus driver who drives our kids to school. I thought, *If he can do it, I can do it.* So I began riding to work — it's about 15 kilometres each way. Some time later I saw him again as I was riding along and I said, 'You inspired me to get riding.' He inspired me and I've inspired others. There's always a flow-on effect.

Now I've got my 13-year-old son Te Hira biking in with me each day. He comes to the clinic after school, and then we bike home again in the evening. It's great exercise for us both and, more than that, it's a chance to do something together, to talk.

You can tell people to get more exercise, but telling becomes like a judgement. *Doing* is far more powerful. I believe that by riding to work every day my son and I are making a powerful statement to fathers and sons in our community. It's a powerful statement of health to say, *Get out there with your kids.* People come up to me and say they saw us riding together, and that's really cool — it's healthy and good relationship stuff. I know it works well for me.

A few years ago I did a Sport Northland survey and realised I was sedentary. Tracy gave me a pedometer to motivate me, and I started going for walks at lunchtime. Then I started running. Even though I'd been quite athletic in college I'd lost a lot of fitness, and when I first started running I could hardly run a kilometre; I could run 750 metres then I had to stop. But I wouldn't be put off. I said to myself, *OK, today I did nearly 1k, tomorrow I'll do 2k and the day after that, 3k.* Before long I could run 10 kilometres, then 20, then 30 kilometres — the round-trip to work and back — not bad for someone with a traditional Polynesian physique, muscular, not lean.

Then I went down to Taupō to watch the New Zealand Ironman event — that's a 3.8 kilometre swim, 180 kilometre cycle and a marathon run of 42.2 kilometres — and I was completely hooked. So for the next year I trained really hard and managed to complete the 2010 Ironman at Taupō in 11 hours and 52 minutes. Since then I've done the Ironman two more times, IronMāori twice, about 10 half-Ironman races and a whole lot of long-distance cycling races. I like cycling and I'm pretty good at it. In my field I'd be in the top half of cyclists, which in an Ironman is quite an achievement — all those alphas. In the swim I'm also in the top half; but my running is pretty slow.

Most of the people who do Ironman racing are people who don't need to do Ironman racing. They're like me: seeking out these adrenaline-loaded events because we are driven people who are a bit crazy and focused on proving ourselves. We're already full of self-belief, already on top of the world. We just want a little bit of a cherry on top.

But probably about 5 per cent of people who get across the line are even more amazing because, until they challenged themselves to do this, they had no self-belief. Their achievements in these races are truly awesome. They'd be the people who a year or two ago were sitting on the couch. Some of the best parts of Ironman happen in the hour before midnight, when the tail end is coming in. These people are the real warriors of the day.

After I'd done my first Ironman I held a session at the clinic where I showed my slides, trying to encourage other people into it. Our office manager, Hinerangi, with a couple of others, signed up for it and she has now done two and a half Ironmans (one year there was a storm and we could only do a half race). Now we have four or five people from Kaitāia who have completed Ironman.

But IronMāori has been our biggest success story. The number of competitors from Kaitāia jumped from one to 45 in a year, and now every year around 50 people participate.

IronMāori is specifically designed to get Māori more active — it's a 2 kilometre swim, 90 kilometre bike ride and a 21 kilometre run. The competition sells out 20 minutes after it opens — it's phenomenally successful and crazy popular. It's successful because the event has tikanga, tautoko and manaakitanga. It's the proof: if you have the right settings and if you have the right message, Māori will take it on.

Things like IronMāori are contagious. We create a buzz, and enlist a few other people who are also good at making a buzz in the community. We tap into people's various strengths, such as being competitive, or getting their whole whānau involved. We try to make it go viral.

Of course, these events aren't for everyone. I encourage my patients to take small steps to get active. It's like when you do a marathon, if you looked at the finish line while you were still at the start line, you wouldn't believe you could get there. But you just take one step at a time.

I have seen people make really good changes to their lifestyles by getting into triathlon and endurance sport, and as they meet and overcome personal challenges, they've built their self-esteem and confidence. I believe that the health system would serve our country better if we invested more in initiatives like this. These strategies have the ability to create more health improvements than the thousands of prescriptions that I write each year.

//

Once Tracy and I started having kids we wanted to be great role models for them. This was very important to us. Tracy did a lot of horse riding growing up but not team sports. Like me she started getting into triathlons and we'd take the kids away to events and they'd do Iron Kids. Tracy did the half-Ironman races, and half marathons. She's not a great swimmer, but has persevered and swum 2 kilometres in IronMāori — a real mean achievement. The girls are good swimmers, even though they haven't really gone down that path of competition. And I'm happy because they have a really healthy level of activity.

Conor's very competitive. He's really got into the challenges and has an amazing discipline and knowledge about fitness and training for endurance. He won the long-distance triathlon championship for New Zealand and did IronMāori with us at 16 — at the time the youngest ever to complete the race. He did his first Ironman at 18. Conor and I have done heaps of triathlon stuff together. It's really cool doing things with my kids and I enjoy it just like I'm enjoying the cycling with Te Hira.

IF YOU HAVE THE RIGHT SETTINGS AND IF YOU HAVE THE RIGHT MESSAGE, MĀORI WILL TAKE IT ON.

A lot of adults who get involved in these fitness challenges do so because they have kids of their own. They want their kids to respect them, and they want to inspire their kids. And, in turn, the kids want to do it because they see their parents doing it. This reminds me of the message behind the One Heart Many Lives campaign — let's acknowledge how important one life is to the people around us. One person can make a difference to a whole family. It's never just about doing it for yourself; it's about doing it for your whole family.

People say, 'Oh, Ironman — that's crazy!' But I like to do extreme things. It's crazy to have seven kids, a busy job and do a lot of training . . . but I love it. I biked from the clinic up to a vMOKO meeting at Ngataki Primary School — that's about 66 kilometres each way.

Someone said to me, 'But won't you be too tired for the meeting once you get there?'

And I was like, 'No! I'll be energised.'

Exercise never tires me. It energises me.

If I can't do exercise, it's a disaster — like when I got my shoulder fixed. I was a grumpy old man, really stressed and down. As soon as I was well enough, I was back out on the road with it strapped up. I've had both shoulders reconstructed — but I'm still playing league at 41. Generally I'm too busy to train too hard, so I just make the exercise part of my regular day, like biking to work.

This is the great part of my job — where I get to see people making positive changes to adopt a healthier lifestyle. I've seen many guys who lose 30 kilograms, they're eating well, they've stopped smoking, and they're getting their kids out for a walk with them. It is achievable. It doesn't require lots of money, but it does require lots — *bucketloads* — of inspiration, determination and support.

//

One October morning in 2013 I attended a meeting of people standing for mayor of the Far North. It was a Saturday and I'd just completed the morning rounds at the hospital, and I made my way to the Te Ahu Community Centre via the excellent Saturday market where I got my ritual coffee and blueberry pancake.

I had an agenda. I wanted to lay down a challenge. It related to the relationship between pokie machines in the Far North district and poverty-related preventable diseases such as rheumatic fever, bronchiectasis, depression, suicides and domestic violence. Would any of these mayoral hopefuls dare to commit to reducing and eradicating pokies from our district? I considered attending this meeting as important as the work I had just completed on the hospital wards.

Not long before, I'd met a researcher in problem-gambling from Hapai te Hauora, a Māori public health organisation, who stunned me with the statistics around pokies in the Far North. Out of the entire Northland region, the Far North has the highest number of pokies per capita, with one machine for every 111 people — that was a total of 341 machines across 28 sites. The ratio of pokies in the whole Northland region was one for every 168 people. But in Kaitāia, Kawakawa, Moerewa and Kaikohe, where around 60 per cent of the district's pokies are clustered, there is one machine for every 45 people.

If we were talking about an infectious disease like swine flu, this would be considered an epidemic.

Each pokie takes about $45,000 per year, and over a single three-month period in 2013, pokies in our district took a staggering $3.5 million. Given that most of these machines are in areas of low income and high need, that is money coming out of communities that cannot afford it. Up to 85 per cent of problem gamblers use pokies as their main form of gambling; and Māori women feature prominently here. Gambling counsellors say some pokies addicts are losing as much as $3000 a fortnight, using crime or credit cards to finance their addiction.

I am convinced that the presence of pokies in communities such as ours causes harm. I am convinced that the people I see who cannot afford prescriptions for their illnesses, electricity for their heating and nutritious food for their children's lunchboxes are victims of this epidemic. I am certain that the presence of pokies in our community contributes to the serious poverty-related diseases I am putting bandages on in my clinic on a daily basis. You could buy a lot of health for $3.5 million in a community like ours.

So I asked those wannabe mayors: 'What commitment will you make to addressing child poverty by reducing gambling harm in the Far North?' I asked if they would support a sinking-lid policy where no new pokies or venues would be permitted, with a move to eradicate all pokies from our district.

How did they fare? Well, I should have stayed in the hospital! The mayor at the time, on whose watch pokie regulations had been diluted, made the comment that $500,000 of pokie money helped build the new Te Ahu Community Centre where we were meeting. He didn't stop to consider how often the people who put their gold coins into the pokies come to the library. Some of the gaming trusts cover a wide area from Auckland to the Cape, so it's quite feasible that Auckland organisations which are well versed in how to apply for funding access grants gained from money taken out of Far North communities. I doubt that Auckland beneficiaries of Far North money ever frequent the dingy, dark gaming rooms of Kaitāia or Kaikohe.

John Carter, who was eventually elected, responded by saying that while he was inherently against gambling of any sort, he would not commit to putting a plug in this poverty drain. However, a year later the council he presides over did institute a sinking-lid policy for pokies — so that's great.

A number of candidates made the disturbing comment that this form of gambling is an individual choice and as a potential mayor they could not do anything about this.

As well as making the point about the damage pokies cause in our community, I want to make a point here about leadership. I was stunned that people standing for a senior public position did not believe that they had a responsibility to influence the community to make it a better place for us all. What a wasted opportunity! Tough smoking laws and a vision for a smokefree Aotearoa have shown us that sometimes we need our elected leaders to make hard calls, and that we all, as individuals and as a society, reap the benefits of them doing so.

I believe that the mayor, or any other elected representative who gets into a decision-making position, can save lives — just like we do in the hospital.

//

The job of health policymakers is to be bold. Just as we demonstrate leadership in the way we live our lives, we need to show leadership when it comes to making tough decisions about our spending priorities. The best way to spend money in the health system is on prevention. It's better to spend $1 now to prevent $1000 being spent in 20 years' time on an individual.

For instance, let's tackle soft drinks. Everyone's going to cry 'Nanny state!', but those people who are crying nanny state are also the ones who are going to come to us in 20 years' time and say, 'I want my hip joint done,' and we'll say, 'I'm sorry, 20 years ago when we told you we've got to stop the tidal wave of obesity-related disease and cost, you said we were being nannyish. But now we're too busy fighting kidney disease, kidney failure, diabetes and so on, and we can't afford to do your hip.'

I believe the health minister should work closely with the education, finance and housing ministers. Because, great, let's get kids a world-class education, but what about the sick kids who aren't learning because of illness? How do we keep our kids healthy so they can get a proper education, so they can get good jobs, so they can contribute to the economy, so they can be part of the workforce?

The answers aren't simple. We need to be courageous. We are leaders: it's our job to be courageous. We might have to stop funding what we've always funded. We might have to stop doing some surgeries that we've always done, because the value we get back from them is not matched by what we're spending on them. It's a really sensitive issue, but perhaps we need to look at palliative surgery. The amount we spend on cancer-related treatment, when the person dies two or three months later anyway, is considerable: $50,000 to keep the person alive for six weeks or two months. But we do this because we've become a society that wants to stretch out people's lifespans. Life at any cost. This requires brave public debate. A personal story involves my father. He led a lifestyle that resulted in cancer. He was diagnosed in late 2013 and went on to have chemotherapy, radiotherapy and surgery. This included admissions to hospital, specialist visits and community care. My dad was given a chance to live, but ultimately this care was futile. My concern was that for the sake of six months, my father accounted for a large amount of health spending. I asked myself, *Could this money have been better spent preventing alcohol abuse, or addressing children living with poverty-related health issues?*

We think, *We can do it, so we must.*

Our health spending is going to blow out in the next 20 years. We have to rethink what we as a nation want from our health system.

What would you like for your mother? She's 85, she's in a rest home, and she's fallen and broken a hip. We can almost guarantee that if we don't fix her hip she'll be bed-bound and will probably die in the next two to four months. Or we could spend a large sum to fix her hip. She still probably won't ever be as mobile as she was. There's a 50 per cent chance of her dying in the next six to 12 months anyway, and if she does survive this fall, the fact that she fell in the first place could make her fall again. Or you could look at some of that money going somewhere else. That dollar value could bring significant benefits to a family of seven in an unhealthy house.

I know it's a hard decision. It's difficult to talk about, isn't it? Yet we need to find the courage to look at the ethical challenges without shying away. The examples I've given are probably the most extreme — but we do need to courageously revisit our health system and the values it reflects. Not facing up to these issues is the equivalent of sitting on the couch with a television remote in our hand and a box of beer at our feet. As health professionals we need to lead by example when it comes to a healthy lifestyle; we also need to lead in terms of our willingness to confront the challenges in our health system, for the sake of future generations.

We could also revisit the idea that everything can be fixed with a pill. I spend way too much of taxpayers' money on prescriptions for drugs. I'll give a person eight medications, which can be at a cost of $30,000 to $40,000 a year, and really what that person needs is a lifestyle coach. He needs someone who will work with him, drill right down and figure out what it is that is making him not get out and walk, and still eat a loaf of bread in the evening with his fry-up and his boil-up, and still pour a ton of salt on each meal, and still smoke and still drink. I can give this guy eight tablets to treat eight different parts of his body, but the one part we need to treat we've got no resource for: his brain, the thing that controls his reasons for doing things — his will and his psychology.

18 // THE WONDERFULNESS
OF BEING INDIGENOUS

Tracy and I feel pain every time we turn on the news and we hear about a violent, impulsive crime. We hold our breath and say, *Please don't let the perpetrator be Māori.* Or a child has died, and we say, *Please don't let that name be Māori. Please don't use the word 'whānau'* — because as soon as that's said we know it's going to be a Māori child.

It's uncomfortably frequent that we see our culture on the front page. Why it hurts is that we're trying to build a bridge between Māori and those in New Zealand who are fearful of us, who don't think we deserve a place, who think we're rabid child killers. These terrible events are a step back.

I think of the Maori Battalion, the great Māori war effort. The purpose of that was to show we had a place in this society. The sacrifice those men made was to show Māori were prepared to make an equal contribution. For a long time we have displayed our willingness to be part of this society, but then sometimes we read about those terrible things and that sets us back in some people's minds.

But I know from 10 years of attending indigenous health conferences that indigenous people all over the world share a history and many scary similarities in their current situations. I listened to an Aboriginal person stand up and talk and I felt his pain when he spoke about his children dying, his people dying before their time. Suicide rates are very high, rheumatic fever rates are high, just because we are indigenous.

IT'S UNCOMFORTABLY FREQUENT THAT WE SEE OUR CULTURE ON THE FRONT PAGE.

And yet there's this shared thing about the wonderfulness of being indigenous. Indigenous pride. The indigenous family coming together. While there are really hard things about being Māori, I would find it really bizarre not to be indigenous. I wouldn't know what to do with myself. Could I be passionate about being the third or fourth generation of an Irish immigrant family? Could I be passionate about a particular issue of relevance to my region, my locality, my family? Could I be passionate about an issue — say, a green economy? I could, but it wouldn't be the same. Because the passion I have for being Māori is a passion that I was born with. It's my heritage.

//

Through my mother's family I was brought up to be Catholic. The Christian faith is a big part of Catholic life, and we spent a lot of time going to church, visiting families after church, praying in the evening. There was great comfort kneeling at night with my grandmother and praying before we went to sleep.

When I went to Hato Petera, that was all enforced, embedded in the way of life. We had chapel every day, prayers and hymns — strong powerful songs, all in Māori — and a wonderful positivity about the culture. Everything I was seeking in my life I got to enjoy every Sunday at Mass. At that stage of my life I knew nothing about Māori spirituality.

However, after I left school and was becoming enlightened about Māori issues, I came to associate the Christian religion with loss of land, because I saw that the missionaries came with the Bible in one hand and a survey peg in the other. True, some individual missionaries opposed the sale of Māori land, but nevertheless, the Church was intricately involved in the colonisation of our people. As we gained Christianity we lost our land and our language and our culture. Wharenui were burnt down because they had carvings deemed offensive to a conservative Western culture. Our people were taught to endure hell on earth to earn a place in heaven. Māori had a pre-colonisation population of probably around 200,000, according to the online encyclopaedia Te Ara, and only 42,000 by 1896, due to war, disease, famine and social and economic isolation.

In 1856, Dr Isaac Featherston, a physician and secretary of the new colony, famously said the duty of Europeans was to 'smooth down the pillow of a dying race'. Just 46 years later it had almost come true.

People will say we were a warring tribal nation before the Europeans arrived. I say, 'Yes, but we still had 200,000 people at the time Captain Cook arrived, so we weren't warring that much. We weren't on the brink of extinction.'

So although I experienced many positive things about Christianity and the Māori Catholic church during my childhood and my time at Hato Petera, I became very anti-religion. I began questioning the place of Christianity — a Pākehā religion — in Māori culture.

But I have always been a spiritual person. When I was a boy and very confused about the material world and all the things that were getting me into trouble, I spent a lot of time on my own, and as a young man I did a lot of hitchhiking around the country. I'd often go into the bush or climb a mountain, and sit there quietly, maybe meditating or praying a little, soul-searching. Right from childhood, I often had a feeling that I wasn't alone.

Later, when I heard people speak on marae, I guess my radar went up: *Hey, he did a karakia that wasn't Christian in its basis.* These karakia were about the old gods and the tūpuna and our connection to the environment, and I liked that. In the last 20 years or so there has been a real resurgence of interest in pre-colonial beliefs, and a renaissance of traditional karakia.

I came to believe that the feeling I'd had of not being alone was the presence of tūpuna, the ancestors who were close to me and guiding me. I became keen to explore more original, authentic and older philosophies around spirituality.

About 10 years ago Tracy and I began the practice of saying karakia at the beginning and end of every day. It's really cool. The kids say, 'It's time for karakia, Dad.' If they haven't had karakia, they say, 'Dad, I had a nightmare last night! Can you do a karakia for me tonight?' So they get into their beds and I do a karakia in Māori, and in the morning I get up and do one — a nice loud one in the hallway — to get everyone in a good mood. Te reo is the first language they hear in the morning and the last language they hear in the evening.

If you are somewhere else in the world you can do your karakia and you're still connected to home.

Karakia are prayers to the supreme god Iomatuakore, and then to the sky father Ranginui and earth mother Papatūānuku, and then to Tāne-mahuta, god of the forests and birds, and all those other gods. We remember our tūpuna. We talk about ourselves and ask for a good sleep to prepare us for the next day. We pray for those who are sick and lost in the sense of spiritually lost, and those who are sad and hurting. We try hard to teach the kids to think about others, so they're not just me, me, me.

Karakia is part of our everyday life. When we go diving we do a karakia to Tangaroa, the god of the sea. We acknowledge him, and we mihi to the children of the sea, asking for protection and guidance while we're out on the rough waters and we promise that we will respect the moana.

But we've also come full circle and have started going to church again, the Māori Catholic church. That's a new development for our family, and it came partly out of a recognition of how good things are for us. I didn't want to just turn to the church when we were desperate; I didn't want to go to church when everything else was failing and we needed something to make us feel better. I've seen that happen a lot. People think when things are bad that the church will make it all better. *No,* I thought, *let's go when things are going great, when everything is fantastic for us. Let's go when we think it could enhance who we are as a family.* So we went back.

I was on a high from being named New Zealander of the Year and getting all these other awards, so going to church was also about getting a bit grounded, making myself humble. It was about listening to the priest, sitting there as the student. I'm not the teacher. I'm not the leader; I'm a passive participant. And it's almost like every sermon is directed at me. The priest is up there talking about the importance of being a good husband, of utilising the skills God has given me to the best of my ability to help others in a Christian way. Those sorts of things, they resonate with me and I find them uplifting.

And, of course, we meet people and have this community feeling. I really love it.

Christianity and Māori spirituality sit very comfortably together for me. I do believe there are some aligned ideas around the idea of supreme beings. We do our traditional Māori karakia in the mornings and evenings, and then we go to church on Sunday and have a purely Catholic-based service. If people ask me to give a karakia at an event, I used to only ever say a traditional Māori prayer, but now it would be quite easy for me to do either, or both.

We need to believe there's something more powerful than us in this world. It can be anything you want. It could be Buddha, Allah, Iomatuakore, God. It could be the environment or nature. But whatever it is, it's important to have a faith. I sometimes say this to patients of mine who are clearly lost in the world. I say it because I believe we need to realise that we're not responsible for everything that goes on. That's quite a burden.

I like the thought that my successes as well as my failures are not just because of me. I believe that my success is due to the fact that I have some amazing tūpuna on my shoulders, and I have some atua who are protecting and guiding me, determining which way things will go. Obviously my wife and my family share my burdens and successes, but as well as them I have rituals that remind me of and acknowledge the role of greater forces than just myself in all the outcomes of my life. I karakia every morning before I go to work, and every day before I get home to my family I do a cleansing prayer. When the water is nice I do it in the lake, but most days I do it with running water, allowing it to cleanse away the very heavy load of being a doctor.

If I didn't believe that there was a power capable of cleansing me, but I just believed that the ritual of washing in water was cleansing me, separating me from the burdens of my day, that's still a faith — and that's my point I make to people. Who or what are you going to reach out to every day, first thing in the morning, to prepare you for the day, and to bring you and your family protection and guidance?

With my return to the Catholic faith, I have been appointed the representative of the Bishop of Auckland, Patrick Dunne, on the trust board of Hato Petera, a position that guards the dual character of the school as both Māori and Catholic. Like other aspects of my public life, it's a job that demands I behave as a peacemaker, as a bridge.

Currently there's a Treaty of Waitangi claim against the Catholic Church, led by some of the old boys of Hato Petera. It has created tension between the church and the school, and I see myself as the peacemaker there, to remind them that we have an important future as Māori Catholics.

In summary, my relationship with religion and the wider interpretation of faith in many ways reflects my journey from a radicalised young Māori who was very anti-establishment to who I am now. I see how relevant religion is for my whānau, and that is a comforting thought.

//

As Tracy and I developed our understanding of Māori spiritual practices, our tikanga, our kawa, around birth evolved. Initially, when we were young parents, we heard about this idea of planting the placenta, the whenua, into soil, under a tree.

'OK,' we said after the birth of our first child, Conor, 'we'll take the placenta home. We're Māori so apparently we're meant to do something with it.'

We placed it in an ice-cream container and put it in the freezer for about two and a half years. Finally, an elder told us we shouldn't have the placenta in with our food because the whenua is tapu and food is noa, so that was another lesson for us. We took it out and buried it under a kauri tree.

By the time we'd had all our children, we had our cultural practice down to a T. We bury each of the placentas on Mokoia Island in Lake Rotorua because that is Tracy's place and it connects all the babies together in the papakāinga, the place of standing and origin. Kia hoki te whenua ki te whenua: placenta back to earth. Then we take the pito — the piece of umbilical cord that eventually drops off a week or so after birth — and bury that on one of the sacred mountains of our tribes, Taumatamāhoe south of Kaitāia, or Kaitarakihi, sacred maunga of Ngāti Maru in the Coromandel.

About a month before Tracy was due to give birth to our youngest son, Lance junior, Conor, Te Hira and I went out into the bush on one of the mountains. We found a nice tree, a ponga, and we cut it in half and hollowed it out. Then we took some whenua, dirt, from our sacred maunga, and we harvested some harakeke. So when Tracy had the baby we were all ready. The pito went straight into the ponga container, which is like a waka huia, a sacred carved box, along with the earth from the mountain. We put the lid on it and tied it up with the harakeke, and as soon as we could, within days, we went back up to the mountain — it's a real mission — and buried it there with karakia and prayer and waiata.

This practice is our perception of what is right. There's no book and there weren't any kaumātua telling us how to do it. We just said, 'This ritual is what we're going to create for our family.' Because part of what we do now is about creating a kawa for the family, a guide by which we can live and which our children can use when they in turn have children. We took our son Wairua back to his maunga — Kaitarakihi — where his pito is buried. We climbed this maunga, which took six hours for the return trip. When we got to the top, we had our karakia, mihimihi and waiata. I looked at Wairua and saw that he was crying. I asked, 'Son, why are you crying?'

He said, sobbing, 'Because my pito is buried here, Dad.' He is a pretty deep little fella, and that was quite a moment for us.

When our children stand to say their whakapapa they can say, 'I have been up to my maunga and I've seen where my pito is, and I've looked over at the awa and the whenua.'

They are connected to the land and the layers of people who have gone before.

19 // MAKING PEACE WITH DAD

My dad, Eddy Watene, died while I was working on this book. He died of oesophageal cancer, which is strongly correlated with heavy drinking. Alcohol took him from me 40 years ago when I was a young boy wanting to see my father, and it has now literally taken him from me.

Over the years I kept in touch with Dad, never giving up on my sense that he was my father and had a place in my life. He moved to Australia some years ago, and he'd ring me when he needed to go to the doctor so that I could help him communicate. Because of his lack of education, and also because of what the alcohol had done to his brain, Dad was a really poor communicator. It could be really hard to figure out what he was saying.

One day he rang me from a doctor's surgery in Melbourne. The doctor got on the phone and explained that Dad had an 'obstructing lesion in his lower oesophagus'. It looked like cancer. I knew straight away that this was bad. Survival rates from oesophageal cancer are really low.

He eventually decided to come home.

'We'll look after you, Dad,' my sister Nikki and I said.

We were so happy we were going to have the opportunity to take care of him. He could stay with Nicky in Auckland during his treatment, then come home with me to recuperate. He would have his kids and his grandchildren around him. It was important to us that we did this together as a family.

It shows how strong that bond is. No matter how poor the relationship we'd had with him, he still meant that much to us. But Dad had other ideas.

___

AS A YOUNG MAN I USED TO CARRY A LOT OF RARU, RESENTMENT, TOWARDS DAD.

'I'm going to Palmerston North,' Dad said. 'I'll get my treatment down there.'

I was at Auckland Airport when I heard about his decision. Essentially, it was a decision to stay apart from us during his final months. I had to have a little tangi, a little cry, while I digested the news. I was bereft.

Oh gosh, it never ends. My dad never stops hurting me. I'm a proud, successful, confident man but I've been hurt by my father and it never stops.

I had a few days like that. I wasn't angry with him. It's true that as a young man I used to carry a lot of raru, resentment, towards Dad, but I had managed to get rid of that a few years back. As part of my quest to improve myself and my outlook on life, to be a better husband, I enrolled in a Landmark course with Tracy. I wasn't thinking about my dad at all, but I learnt that I had this major hang-up about my father, and it was really affecting my ability to be the husband and father I wanted to be. I think it was even damaging aspects of my relationship with my mother. In other words, the resentment and anger and rejection that I was carrying around were shaping all my other relationships. It was good to become fully conscious of that, and I realised I needed to address it.

Dad, I really resent you for not being there when I was growing up. For not being there to protect my mum, for letting us down, for you not being that strong proud Māori father I so desperately needed you to be . . .

So one day during the course I rang him. I was crying. I said, 'I love you, Dad. I love you and I've held on to a lot of hurt for a long time but I'm going to let that go now.'

He was really quiet. He didn't have to say anything because I wasn't asking anything of him. But inside myself I knew I was letting go, and that I was forgiving him. And I wouldn't say I managed to do that 100 per cent but certainly I let go of a great portion of my negative feelings. It was all put to the side.

This whole area of apology and forgiveness is really interesting. There have been times when I've had to apologise to someone in the course of my work. Perhaps I've made a mistake of some kind. Maybe I've behaved impatiently. In one case, a patient had died and I went down to the undertaker to sign the necessary forms, and when I got back to work the undertaker rang me to say he didn't have the forms, that I must have taken them back with me.

'No way,' I said. I got precious, the way doctors can do. 'You're wasting my time, I'm really busy in my clinic, I came down there as a favour to you . . .'

And then I found the papers. I felt really stink. I knew I'd behaved badly anyway, and then found out he was right all along. What should I do? I could've just got my receptionist to fax the papers through, but I knew that wasn't good enough. So I rang and I said, 'That was really wrong and I made you feel it was your fault, so I apologise.'

Apology is partly about asking for forgiveness, but it's also about being clear with yourself about what's right and wrong in your own behaviour. So, by apologising, I felt better about the situation, regardless of what response I got. And it was the same with Dad. In coming clean with my emotions, in admitting my hurt, I felt better, regardless of what he said — which, of course, wasn't anything really. Since then I haven't had the same resentment towards him. Sure, some things continued to annoy me. I still got irritated or upset sometimes. *What a pain.* But I took it less into myself. I recommend it: if there's someone you need to talk to, go and do it.

The awful thing about Dad deciding to die down in Palmerston North was that it was all so utterly predictable. There he'd be, several hours down-country, too far away for us to have anything much to do with him until the very end. We visited when we could but it was such a long way away. And then one day Tracy and I visited him and realised he was very close to the end. Soon after, my sister Nikki made a plan to bring him to Auckland to be with us all. It required some delicate negotiations so that it did not seem like we were pushing him into it. He was so ill we had to charter a plane with a private nurse. We took him to my sister's house and we were with him to the end.

Why did we do it? We had a choice. We could have said: 'OK, Dad, you've made the decisions you've made. You can die down there in the hospice. You can get buried in the public cemetery in Palmerston North and we'll come to your funeral and put some flowers on your grave.' But we chose to say: 'No. We don't want that to be how we remember things. We want to be there.' In some ways we did it for ourselves.

We didn't want to carry the burden of letting him down at the end, or him letting us down.

We had this amazing time. My sister became his primary carer during his dying days. All our kids came down to Auckland and spent time with him. I brought my spiritual strengths along, and we did karakia every night. My grandparents had been Mormon, so when Dad was young, up until when he was a teenager, he had had a very strict religious upbringing. He went to the Mormon Church College in Hamilton. As he was dying, his sisters were gathered around him singing the traditional church songs, and he knew all the words. We'd never heard him sing church songs and never heard him pray, but on his deathbed he did both. He knew the songs, he knew the prayers. It had never disappeared in him; it was just buried beneath a lot of mamae, dysfunction. Buried very, very deep.

Usually with Dad there was little emotion. The only time I've ever seen him cry was when he was dying, and we were all around his bed, singing to him and telling him we loved him.

When he died I really wanted him to have a Mormon service at his tangi. This is all part of my own renaissance around faith. Our father came into this world as a practising Mormon, and he lived a life quite distant to those principles, but he was a very troubled man. I wanted him to leave this world with a blessing from the church that he was born into.

The day before his burial at our marae near Thames, Matai Whetu marae, I googled 'Mormon church' and found there was one in Paeroa, so I drove down there and sat in on the service. Afterwards I asked if I could see the bishop. I explained the situation, and he agreed to conduct the service for Dad. It turned out really special, because one of the church members was a cousin of Dad's and knew the family, so they all came along and did this wonderful service. It was an incredibly moving send-off.

Why did we do all this for a father who had let us down so consistently throughout his life?

The complicated thing about Dad is this. I spend my time trying to improve the quality of life for our people. Every day I see the effects of poverty in my community and among my people — I see dysfunction, alcoholism, family violence. Every day, in my life and with my family, I experience the joy and meaning of connecting with my culture and language, and the strong identity it gives me. I was lost without that identity. I go to conferences where the effects of colonisation are openly discussed, and the terrible statistics relating to indigenous people all over the world are acknowledged as being a consequence of colonisation. Well, here, in Dad, is an absolute example of what we talk about in those conferences. He came from an impoverished family, poor in spirit, poor in material wealth, poor in opportunity. He was alienated from land, language and tikanga. As Mum says, who knows how any of us would have turned out if we'd had to walk in his shoes.

On the rare occasions when he came to stay with my family, he and Tracy got on like a house on fire. He genuinely seemed to enjoy our family rituals. At night when we did the karakia he would come quietly into the room and sit on the floor and listen. I think he loved it. And I believe that despite his initial resistance Dad did appreciate what we did for him at the end.

This is what I said in my eulogy at Dad's tangi. I said that for lots of reasons this tangi could have been different. There was the possibility we might not even have had this service — yet Dad received a blessing from the church that he belonged to. I'm proud of that.

There was the possibility we might not have been on a marae, because Dad had little understanding of tikanga and culture. He had only been on our marae with us two or three times in his life, and that was when Nikki and I pulled together the family reunion and a whakapapa workshop. Dad would probably have been there for tangi or birthday celebrations, but it is fair to say he was not a regular contributor to the marae.

There were times when Dad tried very hard to bridge that cultural gap. Sometimes he would surprise me with stories and knowledge, as if he was holding onto a guarded secret. One time he told me how his father was an expert in the growing, preparation and storage of kūmara. This was a complex process to avoid rodent and water damage. Not getting this right could result in famine for the community.

But although there were these surprising signs of his sense of cultural and family identity, he had brought none of it into his everyday life. There was a real possibility that he wouldn't have had all his family, his grandchildren, his children gathered around him to say goodbye.

So this was the perfect send-off for Dad, and that makes me feel happy.

I feel happy that we did a really good job for him.

HE WAKA EKE NOA

//

A CANOE WHICH WE ARE ALL IN, WITH NO EXCEPTION.

WE ARE ALL IN THIS TOGETHER.

PART 5 //

—
THE
LEADERS OF
TOMORROW

20 // FROM SMALL ACTS, GREAT THINGS MAY GROW

You may never know how your efforts will be received by the world, but you can be certain that the things you do — positive or negative — make a difference, maybe beyond what you intend.

My mum has been to presentations by educator Melanie Riwai-Couch, who because of her circumstances grew up knowing nothing about what it was to be Māori. One day her principal wrote on her school report, 'Ka pai, Melanie' and that one small act of acknowledegment of who she was changed her life. It changed the way she thought about herself, and she went on to do great things. She is now the tumuaki of Te Kura Kaupapa Māori o Te Whānau Tahi in Christchurch.

In my case, I got the opportunity to listen to a Māori doctor for 45 minutes and it made me think: *I could do that, too.*

I also reflect on my good fortune — at a crucial time of my life — in getting a judge who gave me a second chance.

When I was 18 I was out with some mates, and I'd been appointed the sober driver. It was a big responsibility and I took it seriously. On the way home we got stopped and of course I hadn't had a drink all night — but I didn't have my licence on me. I was young and stupid and I tried to give them someone else's licence, and then when that wasn't working and I gave them my real name it turned out it wasn't registered on the Wanganui computer. It was a time when I was trying to decide whether to call myself by my mum's name, O'Sullivan, or my dad's, Watene, and whatever name I gave the cops, it was the other name on my licence. They handcuffed me, took me down to the police station, booked me and I spent the night in a cell. They rang my mum.

'Is his name O'Sullivan or Watene?' they asked her.

'Either or,' she replied.

They thought she was being cheeky. But a lot of Māori have dual names, which reflects the two worlds they live in.

It wasn't a big case, but it wasn't the way I wanted to start out my adult life.

Jeez, I thought. *Charged with a crime! I thought that was all behind me.*

I was bailed and due to go up before a judge. I had decided not to get a duty solicitor who wasn't going to care about such a little case, so on the day I was due in court, I got dressed up really neatly and defended myself.

A LOT OF MĀORI HAVE DUAL NAMES, WHICH REFLECTS THE TWO WORLDS THEY LIVE IN.

Who did I get but Mick Brown, the Youth Court judge who presided over the introduction of a non-adversarial youth justice system. I pitched my case to Judge Brown: I had left boarding school at Hato Petera, was new to driving in the CBD, and my intentions on this occasion were good — to be the sober driver for my mates. He immediately understood that you can have a Māori name and a European name, and he dismissed me without conviction. But he questioned me first.

'What do you want to do with your life?'

'I want to go to university. I want to be a doctor.'

'We don't want a young man with those kind of ambitions starting out in life with a black mark against him,' he said. 'Go forth and do well.'

Many years later, in one of those coincidences that make life so interesting, I was at the Sir Peter Blake Leadership Awards night, where I was about to receive my leaders award. On the very same night, Judge Mick Brown received the Blake Medal, the supreme award. I took the opportunity to introduce myself and thank him. It was important to me to let him know that his decisions made a real difference to the young people who came up before him.

Now it's our turn. As leaders today, we mustn't under-estimate the influence we can have on young lives. Our encouragement, our wisdom, our patience, our guidance can ensure that young men and women are ready, in their turn, to take on responsibilities to help improve the situation for our people.

//

The leaders of today need to begin searching for the leaders of tomorrow.

Māori have heaps of governance experience. Marae, land corporations, Māori health and education providers, iwi, hapū and whānau trusts and committees have all been around for decades.

However, this post-Treaty settlement era, where iwi are receiving many millions of dollars in compensation for the Treaty breaches that economically and culturally destabilised them, brings new challenges — not least of which is that the settlements have a tag of 'full and final offer' attached to them.

We've got one chance to do it right.

The culture of governance in Māori society has never been more important than it is now. As iwi seek the best ways to invest this money, the task is to find the balance between not wasting this opportunity for long-term prosperity and ensuring that the people who are struggling today are able to benefit from tangible, immediate gains from their Treaty settlement. I would be disappointed if iwi were unable to realise some improvement in the day-to-day services that their people need to survive.

It comes back to leadership. The responsibility for these important decisions is going to rest largely with boards and trusts around the country, and these are bodies with a mix of skills. Some have this mix right and others, I suspect, do not.

I have been involved in governance, something of which I have little experience and for which I have never had formal training. We cannot assume that the skills needed for governance are transferable from skills in a different area. Some iwi have the right combination of people of different ages and financial, business, political and cultural expertise, and others do not.

The time for planning strategically for effective governance structures is now. Just like the old days when tohunga would identify those young ones with the skills in weaving, carving or war, our leaders of today need to identify the young ones who show leadership potential and start nurturing them to become rangatira (governors) in 15 or 20 years' time.

Iwi need to hold wānanga for these youth, from the ages of 10 up to 40, where they will be taught the skills to govern. Iwi from all over Aotearoa could come together and rather than just having, say, five teenage Māori from Muriwhenua, they could be groomed as a part of a group of 100 rangatahi from all around the country, coming together to cultivate leadership. Iwi should be among the largest subscribers to organisations like Leadership New Zealand and the Institute of Directors.

//

Tracy and I and the people we work with are leaders in our community, but we in turn are inspired by the leadership of others who have gone ahead of us. For 10 years we've been attending indigenous health conferences, and we have been particularly inspired by the example of the Alaska Native Medical Center. Native Alaskans have autonomy over their health budget, and they have created their own health system. They have state-of-the-art buildings, resources, trained staff and an amazing tele-medicine programme because some of their communities are so remote. They've achieved truly astonishing things — notably, a 50 per cent drop in indigenous people accessing emergency healthcare, and a 53 per cent drop in hospitalisations, both of which are indicators that the preventive and primary-care aspects of their system are working well.

The Alaskan example shows that indigenous people can do a good job when they are left to make decisions for themselves.

For me, the jury is out on what a health system that truly addresses indigenous needs in Aotearoa would look like. Some would say putting all the responsibility for indigenous health onto indigenous health services absolves central government of the responsibility to treat all its citizens equally. Putting the responsibility for indigenous healthcare solely onto indigenous people could create a burden, and it could take decades of work to achieve a successful model. The Alaskan model took 27 years to get to where it is now.

At the heart of the matter is having more control over our destiny — over how services are best delivered to our people — because that is quite different to delivering services to the mainstream. I do think that allowing the indigenous population to manage more of their health outcomes — and that includes not just medicine but housing and education as well — would achieve better results. The Alaskan example shows that self-determination is cost-effective.

Tino rangatiratanga is a concept that creates a lot of emotions in people, yet sovereignty probably would result in Māori doing better, and that would be better for the country as a whole. We know that for every dollar we currently spend on healthcare, in 20 years we'll need five dollars. It's going to be unaffordable to continue delivering healthcare in the way we deliver it now. Everyone seems to agree on that — Treasury and health economists, both nationally and globally.

By 2050 we will spend 65 per cent of the health budget on over-65-year-olds. With our ageing population, and all the many ways we have of prolonging wellbeing and life, there are going to be more and more over-65-year-olds requiring an ever greater part of the health budget. But our revenue is not increasing; we are going to run out of money to do things the way we do them now.

I believe the answer is to increase self-management of health at the individual level. It's all about people having autonomy over their own healthcare, rather than relying on doctors and nurses and specialists.

Prevention is a big part of it, too: we've got to tax alcohol, sugary drinks, high-sugar foods — the obvious things that wreak havoc with health and will therefore impact on our economy.

When government ministers say that 2000 kids are going to cost the country hundreds of millions of dollars in their lifetime, that motivates me to improve the potential and productivity of those kids and the people I'm trying to serve.

WE ARE ALREADY MAKING A REAL DIFFERENCE IN OUR COMMUNITY.

Governments set targets for healthcare, and of course as a medical practice we want to meet the targets that are set — such as cutting the rate of rheumatic fever infection, improving immunisation rates and so on. But in our practice we want to go beyond those expectations and set our own agenda, to meet the needs of the people as we see them, as they tell us, on our own terms. Yes, we are part of a mainstream system and we are government funded. We adhere to the rules — and then we reach into whatever space we can find in which to be creative. I believe that we need to empower communities to identify and address their needs through innovation and capacity building, driven by our passion to serve.

//

I've got a lot to learn about what I'm doing now. Our business is only two years old. In the same period I have won some awards that have put me in a new position, where I also have to learn about being a leader who can influence change. If my job was just to be a doctor, it would be a cinch. If my job was just to have a patient walk in, sit in the chair while

I use my diagnostic tools and skills, use my computer, use my prescription pad, and send them home — that would be a piece of cake. The hard part is challenging how we do things, recognising and challenging unhealthy thinking and the unhealthy environments that people live in.

We can make a difference here in our community, among our people. But how can we make change in society?

Maybe it's by getting into politics. I'm not sure about that at all. That path seems fraught with risk: you compromise yourself. Many people who go into politics with the best of intentions find they can't achieve what they'd hoped because they become part of the machine, the machine of the party or the machine of government itself. Maybe they find they're just a lonely voice in a crowd that's moving off in a different direction. The political landscape is littered with people with the best intentions. There's probably no reason why I would be an exception to that (though there are exceptions; I would name Tariana Turia as one of them).

Getting political isolates and ostracises you from half your people at least. Individuals might support someone who is simply doing good work, but as soon as that person has a colour, whether you're a gang member wearing blue, black or red, or whether you're a suited politician with a blue, red or black tie, all of a sudden things change because you're not a person of the people, you're a person of the party, the group. And people have a natural suspicion that politicians can't be trusted.

In many ways everything I do is political anyway, whether it's health politics, the politics of negotiating with funders — primary health organisations, DHBs, the ministry — or politics among iwi, the politics of being Māori. Local politics.

Our clinic, Te Kōhanga Whakaora, has been incredibly successful. We are already making a real difference in our community, so maybe my best contribution can be made by staying where I am. I think there's a strong possibility that we just might continue to focus on what we're doing well and what we can do better, and grow and expand on that. I'm excited to think that by creating good models of community healthcare our influence can reach out beyond Northland.

I will feel pretty deflated if, in 20 years' time, I'm still a doctor treating the same old problems in this community. It would be disappointing if, in a generation or two or three, after I'm gone, the same issues remain. The whole purpose of our work is to make a long-term difference. We're here to be advocates — people who talk about the issues, people who have a profile and so can influence the hearts and minds of others. In a quiet way, we're protesters. As I said, our protest is getting out and doing the work, challenging our people, our community, our colleagues, our health system, our society and our country.

I think back to those women talking about me in the school staffroom, and I reflect on the distance a person can travel in their life. I really do believe we all have the potential within ourselves to go either way — and that means we have to do everything we can to help young people make the right choices so they can live good, productive, happy lives. I know from my own experience that the right help at the right time can be life-changing.

Of course I have crap days — days when it's not easy to see the achievements; you get those days in whatever job you have. But most days aren't like that. Now, on a good day, while I'm riding my bike to work or on the way home, I feel really blessed that I'm living this life. I'm achieving what I hoped I could when I was training to be doctor.

I'm doing the job I dreamed of doing.

// ACKNOWLEDGEMENTS

Thanks to:

Mum — for your dedication, strength and guidance.
Dad — for connecting me.
Nana and Bren — for your love and example.
Nanny Maggie — for your quiet support.
Tracy — for your leadership, love and support, and our family.
*Conor, Te Miringa, Nina, Te Hira, Wairua, Taikehu and Lance
junior* — for making me whole.
Hato Petera College — for making me walk tall.
David Gilgen — for your inspiration.
Margie Thomson — for your accurate account of my life.
My people — for being my purpose.
Our country — for giving me a chance.